The Spirit of
Sun Myung Moon

Zola Levitt

Harvest House Publishers
Irvine, California 92714

THE SPIRIT OF SUN MYUNG MOON

Copyright © 1976 Harvest House Publishers,
Irvine, California 92714
Library of Congress Catalog Card Number: 76-40677
ISBN-0-89081-028-1

Printed in the United States of America

CONTENTS

45302

Chapter One

Miracle on 34th Street?

Miracle on 34th Street?

I felt their eyes on me for a whole block as I approached the corner of 8th Ave. and 34th Street in Manhattan. Every few yards along the pavement an Oriental was stationed, smiling, friendly, but watchful. Many of them carried clipboards and they were all nicely dressed, the men in shirt sleeves with neckties and the women in comfortable skirts and blouses.

They were "Moonies," I well knew. I was headed for the headquarters of Rev. Sun Myung Moon's World Unification Church, which had recently purchased the New Yorker Hotel. The hotel signs were still up and the Moonies had barely moved in at the gigantic new headquarters building, but the streets were already being thoroughly patrolled. The agents of Rev. Moon were stopping passers-by and engaging them in animated conversations about some material on their clipboards.

I walked very fast and with a determined gaze, hoping not to encounter a street Moonie. I was after the real pros inside the headquarters.

I knew all about street evangelism from my times with Campus Crusade for Christ. We didn't stop the people who walked fast either.

I made it through the cordon leading up to the corner, noticing that the Moonies closest to the hotel entrance did not carry clipboards. As I neared my target it became obvious that a lot of security measures were in effect. A tall American youngster in the inevitable necktie was having a candid conversation with an Oriental who had shoulders like an NFL lineman; the two were watching the hotel entrance with eyes that constantly swept the faces of all those on the street. I gave them a weak smile, causing them both to shift their stances as I passed. I thought to myself, ''Dear Lord Jesus, that guy with the slanty eyes must have a black belt in Karate; don't let him throw me across 8th Avenue!''

I knew that the two had made some signal over my shoulder after I passed because another big Oriental came out of the hotel entrance to greet me. Not too many little Jewish guys with beards just walk up to the World Unification Church, I began to gather, and I was the object of more than a little curiosity.

With a lump in my throat I walked right past the new black belt and into the hotel.

REV. MOON'S PEACE CORPS

I had a pretty good idea of what I would find as I investigated the world of Sun Myung Moon. I had been following the progress of his movement for quite some time, had given my share of dollar bills to his fund-raisers to help with their alleged projects for homeless children, or drug-abusers, or ''missionary work,'' and I had read about the supposed brainwashing and deprogramming horror stories lived out by a few returned Moonies. Time magazine had come out with a very complete article about the goings-on with Rev. Moon entitled, ''The Darker Side of Sun Moon,'' and I had watched a frightening TV documentary about the movement on NBC's ''Weekend'' show. There had also been stories in the Wall Street Journal, the National Observer, and numerous other publications. I was as informed as anyone who had followed the public stories, and perhaps a little ahead of those not familiar with biblical prophecy concerning the end times and false prophets.

In any case, I had no misgivings about what I would find at the hotel. I knew I would confront studied, professional missionaries, totally indoctrinated and totally dedicated. I had no fear of these calm young people abducting me into their missionary plans or pulling off some kind of instant brain-wash on me; rather I feared my own emotions about the issue—I thought I might start blurting forth what I really thought about their thing at an inopportune moment. I had come, after all, to learn firsthand as much as I could without committing myself to Rev. Moon, and to report what I had learned in a clear, unbiased fashion. I had to control myself.

I was frankly a little upset about what I'd read in the Time article and seen in the TV documentary, as well as the various news stories about people who had been through the Moon mill. Apparently Moon's religion is not good for people and some have survived it to say so.

Cynthia Slaughter was on my mind. I had first read her story in my local Dallas newspapers, since she came from nearby Fort Worth, and the Lord had led our paths together once in the course of my work. I'd had a telephone conversation with her about her appearing on my talkshow, "The Heart of the Matter," to tell the story of her conversion to the Unification Church and her subsequent deprogramming by ace unMooner Ted Patrick. Cynthia sounded exhausted with the idea of retelling this difficult period of her life and declined to appear on the show, but my contact with her had made me think.

And there in the Time article she was given most of a page (p. 50, June 14, 1976).

Cynthia's story was considered typical. She had read an advertisement which said simply, ''Sincere, conscientious person interested in the betterment of mankind call this number . . . '' She called and was invited to an interview with ''an organization similar to the Peace Corps.'' She liked the atmosphere in her interview and agreed to attend a weekend retreat to learn more about the work of the organization. ''Little did I know that my mind had begun a journey from which it might never return,'' the article quoted her.

The weekend turned out to be almost non-stop lectures followed by the news that the end of the world was at hand. The Second Coming of Christ was expected imminently, however, and ''the person who had brought these new truths to the world was Sun Myung Moon . . . '' When Cynthia wanted to leave she was told that Satan was responsible for that attitude; he would try to pull her away from the movement because she was one of those who had been chosen to build the Kingdom of Heaven.

Cynthia was driven from the weekend to spend a few days on a farm where the lectures continued. There was good fellowship among those who had been chosen to bring the Kingdom of Heaven at the farm, with much singing and socializing. All present signed up to join the movement.

Cynthia was subsequently admitted to a prayer room graced by Moon's picture, before which she bowed, saying, ''Good morning, true parents'' (Moon and his wife are the true parents of mankind, according to the movement).

Cynthia now resided at a Moon center, rising at dawn for prayers and songs and then a day of fund-raising for Moon. ''Even if we could only wrangle a penny from someone, it was a victory for God,'' Cynthia shudders. ''The more money we raised the more God-centered we were.''

The young people were taken to barrooms until they closed to continue the pan-handling into the night. Cynthia was so worn out by the regimen that ''as I arose in the morning, I would fall against the wall.''

But she raised $3,000 for the organization in 5 weeks time.

At that point she returned home to handle some unfinished business and was confronted by Ted Patrick, whom her desperate parents had summoned. The Moonies had warned her that Patrick kidnapped people, gagged and beat them and tried to wrest them away from the movement.

But Cynthia found Patrick less of a monster than that; he was armed with facts about Moon, documents from Korea attesting to his questionable background, tapes from other deprogrammed Moonies and a Bible. ''Ye shall know the truth and the truth shall make you free!'' screamed Patrick in his eight-hour shouting contest with the confused Cynthia.

The deprogrammer prevailed, at length, and Cynthia Slaughter returned to the world she had relinquished for Moon. ''The months that followed were hard,'' she told Time. ''Adjusting to the outside world again was like arriving on another planet . . . It took a long time to fill the vacuum that had been created inside me. It was like withdrawing from a drug. Since then, I have met many others who have left the movement with the fear and guilt I experienced; their stories are almost identical to mine.''

HEAVENLY DECEIT

The Time article drew a picture of a highly suspicious character in Rev. Moon, but I had seen many of the most negative facets of this remarkable man in previous news stories. New Yorkers are skeptical of his "cadres of short-haired, fresh-faced youths marching and singing together", and "Moon's wealth and his political connections and apparatus are also under increasing scrutiny." The considerable financial backing of Moon's spiritual enterprises is attributable to his interests in many businesses in various countries, and to those innocent street collectors—Time estimates their take at "perhaps $10 million a year, and because his cult is legally a religion, all income is tax free." A Moonie proudly cited, "They told us that our work bought the New Yorker Hotel" (quite possible; the aging structure went to Moon for $5 million).

Time carped about the "weird new world" of Moonie initiates, and that "In order to peddle their wares they may claim to be helping drug addicts, orphans, anybody—since such lies are merely 'heavenly deceit'," according to Moonie doctrine. "In restoring man from evil sovereignty, we must cheat," says the unabashed Moon in a Time-selected quote.

Many converts turn over their bank accounts to the movement and cut themselves off from their families, accepting Moon and his present wife as their true parents. But the true, true parents often fight back to reclaim their children and that's where Patrick comes into the picture. An ex-middleweight fighter and former community relations aide for Governor Ronald Reagan, Patrick is no patsy. He says he has rescued 1,000 youths from Moon and other cult leaders.

Time gave Moon's background in Korea, which casts him as debatable messiah material. The Reverend (born into a Presbyterian family, attended a pentecostal church) claims to have had a vision of Jesus Himself on Easter Sunday, 1936, and the Lord commissioned Moon to carry out the salvation of mankind, which He, Jesus, had left unfinished. Moon left his first wife when she was pregnant and went off to North Korea to preach his gospel. There he was imprisoned on a "social disorder" charge, for proclaiming the imminent coming of the Second Messiah to Korea.

Moon had come at a bad time, of course, and was obliged to flee North Korea when the Red Chinese, instead of the Messiah, arrived in 1950. Back in the South, he started a unique religious organization in Seoul. Time reports, "In those days, say early members of the sect, ritual sex characterized the Moon communes. Since Moon was a pure man, sex with him ('blood cleansing') was supposed to purify both body and soul, and marriages of other cultists were in fact invalid until the wives slept with Moon."

Moon has changed a great deal on these excesses, or at least insists on the perfect purity of his disciples. Time quotes him, "You must keep yourselves pure. If you may have to be stained in some way or another, it is better for you to kill yourselves than remain alive."

Over the years Moon wrote his *Divine Principle*, the extraordinary "Bible" of the Unification Church. In it he finds a task awaiting some 20th century Messiah (Moon has never officially announced himself as this Messiah) to complete Jesus' failed mission of salvation. Jesus failed because he did not marry an ideal wife and begin the perfect earthly family. But the failure was the fault of the Jews, teaches Moon, because they crucified him. For this reason the Jews have a "collective sin." (Moon is very hard on the chosen people of the Bible and is regarded by some as an antisemite. As we will see further on, Moon has replaced the Jewish people with a new chosen people more in keeping with his particular doctrines and the world situation.)

Concerning the Messiah to come via Unification Church,

Moon thinks he is already somewhere among us, born right after World War I in Korea. The Reverend himself would, of course, qualify according to this reckoning, but he has thus far refrained from taking this mantle.

It was a long trip from Moon's incredible church in Seoul to the New Yorker Hotel, but through the years this arcane preacher has shown an uncanny knack at gathering both cash and disciples. He has remarried and now claims over a half-million followers in Korea, Japan, the U. S. and Europe. His wizardry with fund-raising and investments has proved stunningly successful and he is now in a position to put some of his most ambitious plans to work.

The next major projected purchase of the movement is the Empire State Building!

THE OLD REVERSE

With all that in mind, I entered the former hotel with some trepidation and a great deal of curiosity. Hadn't the devotees seen the recent Time article or the numerous reports on their master? Weren't they aware of his opulent lifestyle, his mansion overlooking the Hudson, his generally unmessianic fiscal operations? Did they perhaps hold a slight resentment for their own poor lot in life, their constant exertion for the movement, their hopeless-sounding task of saving the whole world?

Not a bit of it!

I noted as I passed through the doorway that an oriental couple was also approaching. I had seen these young people back up the block before I had associated the clipboards with the Moonies, and I hadn't been sure who was witnessing to whom; they both had that happy-faced, glassy-eyed demeanor. But now I saw that the girl had the clipboard and the boy was following her. A successful sale, I assumed, and I determined to keep an eye on this boy as things progressed.

I was ahead of them at the reception desk inside the entrance and I was greeted by a young lady whose face was filled with wariness. Apparently all of her customers were normally escorted into the place by the street Moonies; no one had ever come in before on their own, I supposed. There was no label on the building as yet, and the main entrance was marked only by a sign that said, ''World Mission Center.''

''Is this the Unification Church?'' I asked pleasantly. ''I'd like to know more about your work if I may.''

She squinted at me with skepticism and then excused herself. She had a whispered conference with a superior away from the reception desk for a moment. When she returned she favored me with that automaton smile I had seen out on the street. ''One of our people will be with you in a moment,'' she told me, but I could see that her missionary manual hadn't covered this kind of case. There were about a dozen people scattered around the room, which had been a former cocktail lounge and restaurant, and I could feel many stares.

Finally, a nice-looking Oriental boy came over to me and introduced himself. He told me he was from Japan and he would be delighted to answer my questions. He motioned me to a booth along the far wall. He carried a clipboard.

As I accompanied him to the booth I noticed the Oriental couple from the street enter and go down a hallway. Apparently they had finished the clipboard stage outside and my fellow initiate was being taken to step two ahead of me.

My missionary and I were seated at a table covered by a white cloth in the booth. He took a paper off the clipboard and said he'd like to ask me a few questions. His English was so broken, however, that I couldn't quite understand his questions, so I took the paper and filled in my answers. My answers were all, "Yes," as anyone's would be; the questions were all of the form, "Are you concerned about your future? Would you like to help make a better world? Are you sometimes troubled in your life?" and so forth.

I could hear a lecture going on through the wall. A speaker was giving quite a harrangue in the next room and I picked up some Bible names as he ranted. I longed to get myself into that lecture but I didn't want to push it.

I liked my missionary, who tried as hard as he could to understand me, and I began to wish I could speak Japanese. He was very sincere, very concerned about me, and obviously wanting to make a success of our meeting. I sensed that he wanted me to make the next move at the end of the questions and I told him, "I'd like to hear more."

He interrogated me momentarily, searching for my level of sincerity. Did I realize that the world was in dire trouble? Would I really commit myself to a workable solution? I truthfully told him that I was deeply committed to a solution for worldly problems. One of the questions had been, "Do you believe in a sovereign God?" and I had of course indicated that I did. He knew he had a good catch in me; perhaps I was a weak Christian and would make a strong Moonie.

I noticed the strength of his sales technique—what we had called in the insurance business back when I was in college, "The old reverse." The old reverse had to do with persuading the customer that he could not go to the next step unless he qualified. People want what they cannot have, and we always pretended our insurance was hard to have.

While we were talking I noticed other initiates making it down that hallway with their counselors leading the way. I was dying to get into the lecture and get down to some nitty-gritty Moon religion. I finally just said so, assuring my missionary that I was deeply interested in hearing what the lecturer had to say.

He excused himself for a private conference over by the reception desk. Everybody seemed to have to keep checking with their superiors, or maybe the irregularity of my case threw off the standard operating procedure. In any case, my interviewer returned, his perpetual smile aglow, and asked me to follow him down the hallway.

He opened the door of the lecture room, which was a small meeting room with folding chairs. He seated me in the back and then excused himself and left. The lecturer stood at the front by a blackboard on which he had written "Adam and Eve," with an 'X' drawn through the names, and likewise with Cain and Abel. I figured I hadn't missed much if he had begun, "In the beginning God . . ."

In front of me a few rows sat the Oriental couple. The boy was having the advantage of his girl missionary constantly whispering in his ear and helping him follow the lecture. I began to get jealous. Why had *my* guy left? How was I supposed to understand the lecture without a whisperer? Did they think that I was mature enough to comprehend the profundities without help? Or was the Moonie girl interpreting the lecture into Japanese or Korean for her initiate? Had the superiors outside at the desk told my guy, "Okay, let him in but don't waste any more time with him. He doesn't look kosher." Or had they seated me over a trap door?

The Bible study was quite elementary and I was free to look around the room at my freshman class. The Oriental couple intrigued me. Maybe they were falling in love and she just wouldn't leave his side until he was completely purified.

Maybe he was a back-slidden Moonie who had to start at the beginning again and she was his probation officer. Maybe he was actually an extremely important Moonie back to check on how things were going at the front, and she was his aide. Or maybe she was very, very tough, and was his bodyguard. Anyone who's ever been to Israel knows that young women can be very lethal, very competent security people.

The speaker was lamenting the lack of love in the early world, where Adam and Evel fell and Cain murdered Abel. Things weren't getting any better by Noah's time either, he told us, and I could only agree. Everybody on the blackboard was getting an 'X' through their name and I had the distinct feeling the speaker was taking us somewhere intellectually. I hoped Abraham wouldn't get an 'X' but he did.

I couldn't concentrate very well on this obviousness so I passed the time studying my classmates. Most were young men, mustached and blond; they would make prototpye Moonies, once they shaved off the mustaches. There were women here and there and one old fellow who looked like they'd rescued him from a long drunk. I was to see afterwards that the class was shot through with Moonies who were there to just fill up the room and to close in on the initiates at the end of the lecture. In truth, they couldn't really be picked out from the others, these Moonies all being Americans, and they were akin to the shills who used to stand in the crowds and give the first dollar for the snake oil at the end of the pitch. If the person beside you jumped up at the end of the lecture and exclaimed, ''Where do I sign up?'' you probably would sign up too.

The lecturer looked like a ''nice young man.'' He wore faded green corduroy pants, a light blue jacket and a red tie. He looked comfortable, out of fashion, and right off an American college campus, which in fact he was, I found later. He was a practiced and effective speaker, raising and lowering his voice emotionally, and sometimes becoming plaintive about the failures of mankind.

But there were annoying mistakes in his Bible analysis. He started to give wrong numbers of years for things, wrong interpretations of characters and a very strange picture of how the human race developed biblically. I didn't so much mind the rounding off to 400 of the 430-year internment in Egypt of the Hebrews, but the Babylonian 70-year captivity somehow got to be 210 years. Job was called a minor prophet and placed among the kings. The chaotic relationship of Jacob and Esau was given as an example of the first real love in the world.

He was writing his figures in a column and I realized after a time that we were going to add up these false numbers and reach some conclusion with them. I began to smell that the Jacob-and-Esau thing was going to be some starting point for these calculations.

Indeed, we finally began to compare the period of Jacob-Esau to Christ, roughly 1900 years, to the period from Christ to the end of World War I, again about 1,900 year. The "400" years the Jews spent in Egypt were compared to the period of early Christianity up to Constantine, who stood up for the church in 313 A.D., actually. The speaker said that 313 years comes out to be 400 when we switch from lunar to solar calendars, which inaccuracy gave me a headache. The most possible difference in a period of that length between the lunar and solar calendars would be about 5 years.

Anyway, we went on to compare the liberation of the early Hebrews with the liberation of Christianity under Constantine. Jesus had been given short shrift as the failed initiator of Christianity, and we were now looking for when the *real* Kingdom might begin. As the Jews had failed to take advantage of the Savior's offer of the Kingdom, the world was stuck with trying to make it happen without him, as I understood the lesson. Jesus would not be returning, actually, but the spirit of Christ, quite a different matter, would indwell some other man someday and we needed to find out when that man might come.

There were good days with Constantine, but not good enough to bring on the Kingdom, apparently. We went on to Pope Leo, Charlemagne, Martin Luther and so forth, looking for a clue to the coming new Messiah. Constantine had been compared to Moses, the liberator; Leo's crowning of Charlemagne to Samuel's crowning of Saul. The speaker compared a 210-year decline of the popes to what he interpreted as the 210 year Babylonian captivity of the Jews back in Nebuchadnezzar's time, and Malachi, called by our lecturer, ''the great reformer,'' was likened to Luther.

All of this had my head reeling. I had been afraid to take notes in the lecture, but the speaker's intention, to find a new messiah for a new Second Coming, had me riveted to his words and I remembered the logic pretty well. I had been shocked by his treatment of Jesus, especially in what he characterized as the bad relationship between Jesus and John the Baptist, just another case of lack of love! John had doubted Jesus, said the speaker, citing that John had asked, ''Are you He that was to come or do we look for another?'' and Jesus had answered in fury, ''Tell him about my miracles.'' The argument was John's fault, not Jesus', to be sure, but anyway, God couldn't start the Kingdom in Heaven in an atmosphere like that, according to the speaker. Jesus' mission had come to nothing, and we now needed somebody new.

That's what our calculations were all about. We were going to figure out just when God would send the new Messiah, and the idea was to compare B.C. with A.D. and determine the time.

JESUS' REPLACEMENT

My worst fears were realized after our comparison of Malachi and Luther. Since Malachi came some 400 years before Christ, and since we had already established (if one accepted the speaker's figures) the principle that history A.D. followed the pattern of history B.C., then God was again going to try bringing in the Kingdom 400 years after the great reformer. Or, more simply, Jesus came four centuries after a great reformer, so the new Messiah was going to come four centuries after Luther.

And, finally, since Luther's big years, according to our lecturer, were 1517 to 1530, we can expect that the new Messiah was born between 1917 and 1930, or somewhere just after World War I. He is alive among us now, according to this doctrine, and is between the ages of 46 and 59, at this writing. (Moon himself is 56 this year.) We did not get an explanation of why the Messiah is to come out of Korea, as the Time article specified, but much more amplification of this lecture was promised if we would come to the subsequent weekend of training at Barrytown, New York.

I was trying to give as much credit as possible to this theory in my mind. It does closely resemble some biblical prophecy, and many students of prophecy do expect a soon return of the Lord (Jesus in person, however). The antichrist is also expected soon, which gave me pause in this atmosphere of redefining the Bible. And finally, the history of Israel from the patriarchs to Christ does somewhat resemble the history of this age, from Christ to this century.

Of course, the elegance of our speaker's theory would be lost if we put in the accurate Biblical numbers of years, starting our reckoning with Abraham, with whom God's covenant was made, rather than with his grandsons. And the concept of Jesus having failed in his mission was intolerable to me as a Christian.

We were left hanging on the thought that the Messiah was among the human race somewhere at that very moment. Someone, somewhere, was about to try to bring in the Kingdom of Heaven. What God had tried to do since the fall of Adam and Eve—what Jesus had failed to accomplish—was now to be done, in our time.

It was a mighty exciting thought, of course, and the people were galvanized with the possibilities. The room was electrified as the speaker left off, promising more amplification at Barrytown, if we would only sign up for the coming weekend.

At that moment the Moonies in the room, seemingly every third person or so, left their seats and began talking it up. The fruitful clipboards came forth, this time producing applications for the coming weekend. Everyone was being asked, "Do you want to help bring in the Kingdom of God? Shall we count you in? Won't you help us?" And I heard assurances of much fine fellowship over the weekend, singing, socializing and the whole routine reported by Cynthia Slaughter. I saw some initiates signing up.

Forgive me if I tell you that I slowly came to a boil.

I didn't want to show animosity, I didn't want to reveal my true position as a believer in Christ. I didn't want to blow my cover, in a word. But in that last moment I just became completely fed up. Here were a roomful of biblically unread young people swallowing whole the entire apostasy, the tripe about the Lord's failure and a new Messiah, and I just began shaking my head, "No, No, No!"

The speaker saw me at once and asked kindly, "Do you have a question?"

I really let him have it!

Chapter Two

Moon Madness

Moon Madness

My question was put in a loud, clear voice: "You're not telling the truth about the Bible. Why is that?"

There was a very slight change in the room at that point, a momentary pause. The Moonies who were registering the initiates for the weekend looked up, and some of the initiates looked at me quizzically. Then all eyes turned toward the speaker at the front. His smile broadened.

"There are many ways to read the Bible, my friend," he said calmly. "Many interpretations are possible."

"The Babylonian captivity was 70 years," I retorted. "I'll show you the verse in Jeremiah. And the sojourn in Egypt was 430 years. You changed both of those numbers to make them fit your system. Why did you do that?"

He smiled even more broadly and began to nod at me as if to say, "I'm delighted with your questions; you're a very smart boy." But he said instead, "Why don't you come with us to Barrytown this weekend. All your questions will be answered." He fairly smirked with confidence.

I pressed on, feeling myself get overexcited. "You're purposely lying to these people," I spat out. "You call Job a prophet, you call Malachi a great reformer, you call Jesus a failure. You don't know your Bible and you *know* that you don't! You just say whatever is necessary to get these people off to your brainwashing sessions!"

I had gone too far with that one. The people throughout

the room were following the discussion very closely and I had the feeling that my side was losing somehow. It was not the facts, of course, where I knew I was right. It was that devilish calm of his. The listeners were becoming convinced that I was one of those awful Christians whose intolerance had made it necessary for Moon and Co. to go to all this trouble to bring in the Kingdom of Heaven. I could feel people thinking, "Why does that bearded fellow act so unfair; our speaker is a nice guy."

The speaker left the podium and walked toward me, still smiling. He said, "Why don't you and I talk privately?"

I thought, "Oh, oh. He's going to call in the goons from the street and they're going to kill me on the spot."

But the speaker only took me aside at the back of the room and continued to debate the issue with me. To my frustration, the initiates went back to their application forms and everything was business as usual, as though I hadn't spoken up at all. The speaker intended to keep me occupied until the damage was done.

He engaged me in a friendly discussion, beginning with, "You're quite a Bible reader."

I kept telling him where his mistakes were and he kept telling me about the "room for interpretation" of the scriptures. I conceded that people had different ideas about the Bible, but numbers were numbers and personalities were personalities. His characterizations and his calculating were simply not sound. His estimation of Jesus as a failed Messiah and his expectation of a new Christ were typical apostate maneuvers. "Nobody can read the Bible and find Jesus Christ a failure," I wrapped up. "The Bible says He's coming back and that's all there is to that. Men fail, but God doesn't change His plans."

Obviously I was getting in the way and the Moonies

weren't accustomed to, nor interested in biblical discussions of any gravity. Their pidgin version of the Scriptures served their purposes and they weren't willing, or able, to change it.

As we talked, a pleasant-looking American Moonie girl came by, listened to me sympathetically for a few minutes, acting like a psychiatrist confronting a hopeless case, and then smilingly invited me to Barrytown. She gave me a womanly look that penetrated and seemed to say, "You *could* be quite a man if you would just learn the truth." She must have gotten applications with this timeless routine.

The speaker gently took my arm and invited me to accompany him out of the room. "Where are we going?" I asked warily. "Just to the book table," he said. "Have a look at our books. We're proud of our literature. It explains a lot."

I jumped at this opportunity, not knowing that Moon's philosophy was so easily available. I hated to leave the room while there was still a chance that my attitude might get some initiate to decline the weekend, but obviously I had worn out my welcome. And I was fascinated that the speaker still thought I might be maneuvered into his way of thinking. I like a good argument, and I was loaded for bear.

MOON'S "BIBLE"

Out at the book table my companion's attitude took quite a change. He was no longer really friendly. He became bored, sighed a lot, looked away from me as though there were many more important things to do, and generally let me know that I was too far gone for saving.

Now that he had gotten me out of the room where the critical work was going on he wanted to ditch me. It made me lose interest in the books and in everything else but trying to straighten out this apostate. I just didn't want to buy anything at that place once I saw that this "missionary" didn't care if I lived or died, as long as I quit rocking their boat.

I took a new tack, challenging him about the methods of his organization. "What about the brainwashing?" I asked. "You get these kids up there to your farm and you fill their heads with all this tommyrot. You put them to work for you getting money for Moon. How do you justify that?"

He acted as if he didn't know what I was talking about. He said, "Our conversion procedure is essentially the same as that of any other religion. Our people work at their tasks just the same as any other religious people do. We teach them, we convert them, and we give them a mission. Accusations about brainwashing are ridiculous. Come to the weekend and see if we brainwash you."

I said, "Your workers tell lies about what the money is for. I've given Moonies dollars for all kinds of projects your organization doesn't even engage in."

He told me, "If our fund-raising people tell you a lie they're not doing their work properly."

"What is 'heavenly deception'?"

"I don't know."

I said, "Come on, you read newspapers. You watch TV documentaries. The dishonesty is very well known."

He sighed, looked over my shoulder and offered me the books again. He told me that I would understand everything better if I would be willing to study. He picked up a black-bound copy of Moon's *Divine Principle,* made to look like a Bible, and challenged me to read it. He said, "Rev. Moon has made his inspirations very clear in writing. You're welcome to study his conclusions."

I asked him what he thought of Moon's mansion and his high living. He answered, "Rev. Moon's living quarters belong to the organization and are used for meetings and various functions. His home cost about five or six hundred thousand dollars, but he occupies only a small apartment in one part of it."

I'd heard that sort of yarn before, sometimes in a Christian connection, but I let it go. I began to leaf through *Divine Principle*, and he seemed to approve of that. He honestly seemed very like a Christian witnessing to a tough case. He had put his "word of God" right into my hands and he was now wanting me to absorb some of it. It might convert me after all. Perhaps he thought, "Rev. Moon's word never returns void."

I asked him about Jesus' Second Coming and whether Moon's book explained it. I told him that I expected Jesus Himself, not some other Messiah, and that I could easily show myriad Biblical passages to that effect. Our same Jesus would return, I said, with the nailprints in His hands.

"On the clouds?" he asked me, incredulous. "Do you expect a man to come out of the clouds and save us?"

"Sure," I said. "The Bible says so."

He patiently opened *Divine Principle* to a passage that might cure me of my delusions. He explained to me that clouds are really water, after all, and then he pointed out that Rev. Moon explained that biblical references to bodies of water really meant masses of people. Moon referred to a scripture in Revelation that did make the sea an image of masses of people (Rev. 17:15), but I couldn't help thinking about the Revelation passage that says, "And I stood upon the sand of the sea, and saw a beast rise up out of the sea . . . " (13:1). The speaker's point, as explained by *Divine Principle*, was that God was indicating that the new Messiah would come out of the masses of human beings already on the earth, out of the ''oceans of people'' as it were. Clouds were water, water was people, the Messiah was coming out of the clouds indeed, and so He would be coming from among the people.

I couldn't get my voice back for a moment. Finally I just said, ''That's the longest stretch for a biblical symbol I've ever heard of. If you go that far you may as well throw your Bible away.''

He just referred me to a further passage in Moon's book that admonished everyone to read the scriptures with the proper inspiration, i.e., Moon's inspiration.

I began to see that we weren't going to get anywhere standing there at the book table and trying to take apart the Bible. I was intrigued that Moon would go after such passages concerning the return of the Lord and reinterpret them, but my companion did not really have enough biblical essentials in his head for us to progress. Or rather, his head had been filled with a redone Bible, written to a purpose.

I had wanted to talk to a real pro, and I certainly had one on my hands.

I asked him where he got his biblical training to begin with and he said he was a graduate of a Catholic college. He had majored in medieval history, he said, and he pretty well understood the way the world was going. He said his conversion to Rev. Moon's doctrine had changed his life and he now felt that he was on the right track to bring in the Kingdom of God.

I believed he meant it. I believed that he thought he was right and I knew I wasn't going to be able to change him there and then. Our discussion was winding down into a comparison of personal testimonies. I gave him mine and he thought it was ludicrous that a Jew would believe in Christ, but he just shrugged as if to say, "When a man is caught up in evil anything can happen." He looked as if he wished he could get the truth into my heart.

He finally excused himself, telling me that other work awaited him. He fairly begged me to buy the *Divine Principle*. "It's five dollars," he said. "Do you have five dollars? It's really worthwhile."

I demurred, not realizing that I had been offered an unusual privilege. This book is normally very hard to buy.

RUMORS OF WARS

I left the Moonie headquarters glad to see the daylight again and wishing the Lord would come there and then, *out of the clouds*! I realized these Moon people were going to do some damage in the world and they already had a pretty good start. The New Yorker Hotel is on a great corner, I thought, as I looked around outside. Penn Station, Madison Square Garden and the New York Post Office were virtually across the street. We were in the shadow of the Empire State Building. Millions of passers-by would be contacted directly by these expert apostates in a short time. The lecturer within would grow hoarse day by day as the clipboards came out and the young people were spirited off to Barrytown.

They had a very good thing going.

But my real purpose on this trip was to attend the Christian Booksellers Association convention in nearby Atlantic City, New Jersey, and I looked forward to that activity with great relief. I shook off the laments about false prophets that crowded my brain and made ready for CBA.

At CBA, however, I got no respite from thinking about Rev. Moon and his plans. Nobody is more interested in or more watchful of false doctrines than the Christian evangelicals, and Moon had achieved a place in their thoughts. Cults come and go all the time in this world, and most of those which flourish for a moment fade into quick obscurity. But to give the Moonies their due, they were a topic of interest among the publishers and booksellers at CBA.

Each time I mentioned my visit to the Unification Church I gathered immediate listeners. The Christian people had a great many questions about what was transpiring at the New Yorker Hotel. At length I had a serious discussion with a publisher and that, in a word, is how this book came to be. I determined to make a second visit to Moon's headquarters and try to come out with those books along with copies of his speeches, and to simply report them to the true Church.

Truth to tell, I didn't much look forward to it. I supposed that the Moonies would think I'd ''got religion'' if they saw me again, and I was afraid I would get involved with further teaching and further pressure to go on with the weekend procedure.

But like the rest of the Christians I talked to, I myself was convinced that it was time to throw a little light on Rev. Moon.

I packed with some misgivings and headed back to New York.

"MY APPROACH TO THE BOOK TABLE"

This time I was able to see the Moonies doing a land office business. I hadn't put together in my mind the fact that the Democratic Convention was in progress in Madison Square Garden and the proximity of those extra 25,000 out-of-towners to Moon's nerve center. Things were really jumping in those streets.

I arrived at 7:30 p.m. in the incredible scene of thousands of policemen, endless wooden barriers, Democrats hustling into the Garden, celebrities arriving in limousines, monumental traffic jams, pickpockets, prostitutes, panhandlers, mobs of New York commuters, sound trucks, picketers, radicals, nuns and so many Moonies that I thought I was in downtown Tokyo or Seoul.

It was virtually impossible to walk along the pavement; the crowd just dragged everybody along with themselves. Parked in front of the New York Post Office was a sound truck and powerful lighting, and a speaker standing on top of the truck screaming, ''Stop the government spying!'' This speaker was to go on into the night, appealing to the Convention delegates and adding to the general confusion.

TV crews were everywhere, with the huge vans of the major networks blocking the streets almost completely. Cops were routing traffic around waterfalls of people pressing into the streets, and I thought of Moon's reckoning of the sea as masses of human beings.

And everywhere in that crowd, at least every 10 yards, there was a Moonie with a clipboard.

Now they weren't going at it quite so energetically as they had on that quiet previous Sunday, I could see. It was a little hard to just stay together mentally in that enormous crush of humanity, let alone witness to passers-by about religious principles. I spent some time Moonie-watching and I began to think the zealots had met their match. They looked scared, alone and discouraged, though the pluckier ones were still trying to give their pitch to the bustling crowd.

After I had walked around the several blocks of pandemonium I began to realize that Rev. Moon had summoned a veritable army of disciples to confront this mass of lost ones. Where on earth had he gotten all these people?

It just seemed as though that entire massive mob of innocents were completely surrounded and shot through by Moonies, effective or not. And I realized that the hotel was going to be quite a different matter this time around.

I was right about that. The little former cocktail lounge was mobbed. It had certainly never seen business on this scale before, and the Moonies had their hands full. Every booth was taken by a Moonie and an initiate, and everyone was presumably swearing to his concern about the future, etc. There was a long line of people waiting in folding chairs to be taken to a booth by an interviewer. I imagined that my lecturer friend would be exhausted trying to teach his version of God's Word to all these people.

Even with the odds so heavily against them (crowd scenes obviously weren't very good for street interviews and questioning) the Moonies were bringing the customers in wholesale, and their very efficiency gave me pause.

The Moonie security seemed as tight as the convention security across the street. The big-shouldered guys were pacing up and down outside the hotel entrance and the tall American boy was still at his post, seemingly supervising the operation again. I walked the gauntlet as before and confronted the young lady at the reception desk.

She was in pieces. She was a peculiar girl with a pretty American face and an Oriental accent, my first experience with such a combination, and she was being badly overworked. Her smile was losing a lot of its radiance and she seemed about to stand up and shout, "This is no way to bring in the Kingdom of Heaven!" In any case, she was friendly enough to me under the circumstances, but extremely cautious. Everybody—Moonies, Democrats, cops and commuters—feared a bomb around every corner, and my reception girl was on edge.

I just routinely said, "I was here Sunday and I've decided I'd like to have some literature about your movement."

It was another first for her. Back to the drawing boards. She excused herself to have the inevitable secret conference with an unseen superior and people were lining up behind me. Everything had to be done by the book here, apparently, but I couldn't see the value of offending a return customer. After all, I came with money to purchase books; I should have brought someone from CBA with me to tell them how to run a bookstore.

She was back in a moment with an insufficient answer and she had to make a lengthy telephone call to get further advice. I could imagine her talking with Moon himself, and Moon saying, "He wants to read *what?*"

The first telephone conversation didn't completely solve the question of whether I would be permitted to buy books and there had to be another. I was tempted to tell her, "Jesus will be back before you even get a ruling on this," but I stood there smiling. Everybody smiles at Moonie places, in my short experience, so why not smile?

Finally a higher ranking Moonie appeared at the desk and asked me why I wanted to buy the books. He took me off to one side, a staple of their operations, I gathered. I told him I had attended the Sunday lecture and wanted to know more about the movement. He shrugged and invited me to just attend further lectures. "There will be a lecture starting in a few minutes," he told me. "It's better that you learn through lectures." And he tried to lead me down that hallway.

I asked him why it was better for me to learn through lectures. Moonies don't like questions. They have a way of doing things. My new interviewer, harried as he was by the firesale business going on, took the trouble to tell me that

Rev. Moon's books were extremely profound and could be easily misunderstood by those without proper grounding. Like everyone else there, he seemed absolutely sincere. Lectures were their way of explaining their doctrines.

I told him, "Sunday my lecturer was practically begging me to buy the books. What has changed?"

"Who was your lecturer?" he asked suspiciously. I began to see that they didn't believe that I had been there Sunday, and the whole staff was new. I described my lecturer as best as I could—especially his costume which I supposed anybody would remember.

Then he wanted to know how it was that I'd had a private conversation with my lecturer. Why was the lecturer urging me to buy the books? Normally the next step would be Barrytown.

I didn't want to go into the lengthy discussion I'd had with my lecturer, nor our differences. My private theory was that my lecturer had thought, "This guy has possibilities. I'd like to get him on the team." I was about to tell my new interrogator that I must have a lot of talent for Moonie stuff when I heard a very suspicious voice behind me. There was a quick whispered question behind my back, "Who's the guy that wants to buy the books?"

I didn't turn around. I knew very well who it would be and where those phone calls had gone.

Suddenly I was permitted to approach the book table and everything was settled. There were no more questions. I sneaked a look over my shoulder to confirm my theory of who it was that had come all the way in from the street to approve the unusual case. I was right—it was the tall American, the security chief. He'd probably told his subordinates, ''Yes, he was here Sunday. I don't know what he wants but go ahead and sell him the books.''

I had to give them credit. They had a phone system connected to the tough guys outside and everyone who walked into the place had been carefully observed previously. It was like a flight on El Al.

So I had made it to the book table, at last, but it had almost been picked clean by the big crowd. There were plenty of books left, especially books containing the public speeches of Rev. Moon, but the *Divine Principle* was gone.

A young lady came along to serve me at the book table and I asked at once for a copy of the movement Bible. She said, ''How many lectures have you attended?'' We went back through a little of my qualifications to read the works of Moon so that she could be satisfied, but she still demurred about *Divine Principle*. There, it struck me, was a real difference between Christians and Moonies. We show our Bible gladly and all are welcome to read it.

My saleslady assured me that the other books quoted liberally from *Divine Principle* and that I would learn a great deal from those. I ended up buying all of her titles, and leaving her with five extra dollars and my address so that she could send me *Divine Principle* when they had more stock. I am looking forward to receiving it.

I spotted my original lecturer across the room and I think we momentarily caught each other's eye. But we were both of the same opinion about more talk, I guess—''I've had it with *that* guy.'' We didn't nod or try to meet.

GOD'S HOPE FOR AMERICA?

With my arms loaded with books, and with literature about the Barrytown weekends and other highlights of Moonie life, I made for the door. I had quite a bit of research material now, if not a fairly thought-provoking personal encounter with the headquarters organization. My saleslady had given me a complete copy of Moon's Yankee Stadium speech, ''God's Hope for America,'' given June 1, 1976, and sundry other items of his lore that turned out to give a very complete picture of the man, his organization, and his obtuse doctrine.

I was exhausted, but certainly glad to have gathered my material without enduring the whole Moonie initiation routine. I thanked the Lord, very literally, for providing what I needed, and I appreciated that the indicting research I walked out with was very hard to come by.

I could understand, after some study of these books, speeches and other in-house literature, why they normally insisted that only thoroughly indoctrinated people read them.

AMERICA THE BEAUTIFUL

Somehow I was never so glad to see a New York traffic jam as I was when I left Rev. Moon's 34th Street headquarters. It was like re-entering the land of the living.

All the cacophony of the street was welcome after my tense scenes with the Moonies. There was the guy on the huge speaker truck, his lights blazing now in the dark of the night; he was shouting about America being a police state.

An enormous sign was erected beside the truck saying, "Stop the police state!" The sign was guarded by a cordon of husky New York policemen. The speaker himself had free reign over the crowd if he could manage it.

Nobody asked him how many lectures he'd heard about America, police states, etc. Nobody wanted to involve him in their movement. Nobody wanted him to go away for the weekend so he could learn their doctrine. And he made no such requests of his listeners either.

He was free to think what he liked and say what he liked, right in front of the Democratic Convention.

God bless America! It was good to be home.

Chapter Three

The American Dream

The American Dream

Nobody honors America more than Rev. Moon, to take him at his word. We must almost blush as Moon states that this nation is God's new chosen people, we are all a group of Abrahams, and the future of the entire world depends on the United States saving it.

Moon is here just in time, though, because America is in a terrible decline. God is about to switch to some other chosen people if we don't wake up. God changes chosen peoples all the time, according to Rev. Moon.

Moon's ''God's Hope for America'' speech, which he has given many times (but never so appropriately as during this bicentennial celebration), explains his philosophy about God and His earthly ''champions.'' The early pilgrims were moved, like Abraham, to leave their land and come to a new continent, a ''promised land,'' in order to sanctify the whole world. This is a pattern used by God many times, according to Moon, initially with the children of Israel who failed in their mission.

Moon characterizes the pilgrims truthfully and beautifully in this speech. They were Christians seeking freedom of worship; they were the Godly, oppressed by the Godless. They raised a cry of protest, strong and true, upholding the principles of the Protestant Reformation, and they dreamed a wonderful dream.

Those opposing the Church of England, and enduring its

persecution, first fled to Holland, but Holland did not prove to be the Promised Land they sought. They risked their lives to journey across a great ocean and they settled in a free but savage land. Many had died along the way; the journey was arduous and cruel. But many zealous ones survived to settle this great new land.

AMERICA—THE CHOSEN OF GOD

Moon says that God has a historical pattern when He chooses a people. Abraham was told by God to travel to a distant land and the patriarch faithfully left his homeland to seek God's will. The history of the pilgrims in their new land is made a parallel with the history of the children of Israel by Moon. Significant to the pattern is the fact that God calls people to leave their own soil and settle in a new, foreign land. Among strangers, both the ancient Jews and the American pilgrims established a community for God.

Throughout history, says Moon, God chose various peoples in this same way to champion His cause. As one champion fails, another is chosen to receive God's blessing, and so it goes. (It is sometimes difficult to find examples of Moon's reasoning in the Bible or in history, but in this section we will just review how he builds his case for America.)

God wants to combine church and state to His glory, according to Moon, but Israel failed at this. Christianity replaced Judaism and the Roman Empire replaced Israel in God's new hope for the world after Jesus' mission. The Roman Empire was supposed to combine with the papacy, and the Romans and the popes could have gone forth together to bring the world salvation. But the papacy fell into irreverence, as had Israel before it, and the blessing was withdrawn from Rome.

The Dark Ages resulted from all this irreverence, according to Moon, and God's next try was with the British. Had only the British Protestants been able to combine with the British Empire, we might have then had true world salvation, but again the divine call was misunderstood. God had multiplied the blessings of the English people until they controlled a vast empire, but they lost it as time went on, for not following God's will.

The Protestants fled to this continent for a new try at combining Church and state to glorify God. Now God switched his blessing to the Americans, and soon this country was enriched and enlarged. But we may well go the way of the British Empire, according to the speaker.

Christianity and the United States are now supposed to combine to accomplish Moon's "One world of God." And America has been the new country chosen to receive the coming Messiah. The world will be saved in this century.

Moon's ingenious number systems come into this scheme of things. Christianity had to endure 400 years of persecution at its inception to pay back to God what was owed for 4,000 years (?) of Jewish apostasy. America has now served a 200-year period of preparation to pay off the past 2,000 years of failure and irreverence after Christ.

But now, Christianity and the United States are in a position to create a new one-world system, "with all the nations joined into one," in Moon's words.

GOD VS. THE INDIANS

Originally the American pilgrims had to contend with local pagans, even as Israel did at the beginning of their ministry for God. Many pagans lived in Canaan and the Jews struggled with them, shielded by God and blessed by Him all the way. So it was with the pilgrims; God gave them victory over the Indians because ''America first belonged to God,'' and God had plans for it.

Moon compares the settling of North America, so abundant and successful, with that of South America, not nearly so successful. Even today, South America remains a continent of underdeveloped nations, while North America enjoys constant increase. Both were fertile lands, says Moon, but they were each settled with a different motive, and therein lies the distinction. The pilgrims sought God in North America, but the South American settlers were looking only for gold.

So God cleared away the Indians, blessed the crops of the pilgrims, established the American government ''under God,'' and continued to nurture this new promised land and its chosen people. It is no accident that our coins say, ''In God we trust,'' or that our former leaders were believers in God. We are all part of a master plan of God which, though it has failed before, can now be brought to consummation.

GOD'S COUNTRY

It should be clear that Moon sees America as the stewards of God—the deposit holders of His wealth and blessing. The worldwide Christian Church is impotent, according to Moon's theory, without a nation to combine with, and America must exist for the whole world.

America must realize her mission and not just live for herself alone. This nation was conceived in a sacrificial spirit and that sacrifical spirit must now go on. The champions of God have one characteristic in common—''denial of self.'' The individual American must act sacrificially and the nation as a whole must sacrifice itself for the whole world's sake.

The world will only be saved through unity of the world, and America must step out and lead the world toward that unity. America is God's base in the world today, conceived and built to serve the will of God. Americans must be humble and reverent; we have been called to great things.

If we do well, according to the speaker, ''America will endure forever!''

Above all things, America must not repeat the mistakes of Israel, the Holy Roman Empire and the United Kingdom. America must succeed in creating its own inner unity between the church and the state, and finally lead the world toward global unity of church and the states.

The unification of the whole world has always been God's goal, Moon says. His original blueprint and design was to have unification on all levels among human beings—personal, national and worldwide. His past individual champions—Abel, Noah, Abraham, Jacob, Moses, Jesus—all failed through some irreverence around them to bring in the world restoration. Essential to God's plan for men is world salvation through one family, one people, one nation, one world.

God's best try for this was the coming of Jesus to Israel, but the Jewish people crucified their Messiah and so failed to consummate the salvation of the world. Thus God rejected the Jews and took away their chosen people status. He picked Rome next, and then Great Britain, but again the nations failed Him. Now he has picked America.

None of the nations mentioned has seemed to understand God's will. The English people could have founded the literal ''United Kingdom,'' transcending all national barriers, but religious persecution and a failure to unite church and state disqualified them. The personal greed of the people was also a factor; the English were not sacrificial in spirit.

America must now understand, says Moon, that complete cooperation and unity between religion and state is God's formula, and this country's mission is very clear. We must receive the Messiah for the sake of world unification.

We can be the country to complete God's 6,000 years of planning. We can bring in the Kingdom of Heaven, right here.

THE DECLINE AND FALL OF AMERICA?

But America is not going to bring the world anything but heartache if we don't straighten ourselves out, and quickly. God will take away His blessings if we don't wake up to His will. He has changed chosen peoples before and He will again.

It is no accident, according to Moon, that America has been struck by tragedy after tragedy recently. We enjoyed a golden age when we used to sacrifice ourselves for others, but now we're becoming greedy and selfish. The spirit of America has declined recently—leaders have been assassinated and the morals of the country are slipping. "This is God's warning," says Rev. Moon.

America is the world's defender and the cross is symbolic of our position in the world today. On the right-hand side of Jesus is America and on His left is Communism. The thief on the left did not trust Jesus, but the thief on the right said, "Do you not fear God?" We Americans must say to the thief on the left—the Communists—"God exists, God dwells with *us*!" But we have not done that.

Jesus told the thief on the right, "You will be with me in Paradise." That thief defended Jesus and forgot his own impending death. Americans must do the same, preaches Moon.

But God may be leaving America now because we have not acted fast enough. The world faces global struggle and America is not standing up to the Communists. We have so many devastating problems now—drugs, divorce, juvenile crime. God may be getting off this sinking ship.

And without God things will get even worse.

Rev. Moon describes the city of New York, where he lives, as immoral beyond belief, and crumbling. He laments the immorality of California. Is this what God wants for America? he asks. "God is leaving your homes . . . your society . . . your schools . . . your churches—God is leaving America!"

THE FAILURE OF AMERICAN CHRISTIANITY

Rev. Moon finds great fault with American Christians.

The time for the arrival of The Lord of the Second Advent is near, and American Christians should be God's champions. But these Christians are too busy pursuing their own individual interests and their denominational ties.

The goal of God, Moon says, is not the salvation of any one church or nation—it is not just Christians whom God wants to save, or just Americans. Rather, God will sacrifice His special church and His special nation for the sake of the rest of the world. The will of God is to sacrifice the lesser for the greater.

When Christians become God's champions, says Moon, their own salvation is guaranteed. But Christians must not think only of their own salvation and their own well-being. This could not be in accordance with God's will. A Christian thinking only of his own salvation or that of his own family is not worthy of God's blessing. Personal benefit is absolutely against God's will, according to Moon.

Moon reckons the Christian population of the world as about one-seventh of the total population, and the truly devout Christians as only a very small portion of those. But Christianity is God's chosen religion, and the Christians must now realize that they are responsible for the salvation of the entire world.

God is not really impressed with how many Christians live in America. "The standard is the quality of Abraham's faith," according to the speaker. How many Christians are really crying out for God, putting God first? How many are making God's work their own work?

America must have churches filled with faith—"fiery faith." Instead, America's churches are becoming homes for senior citizens. American laws have struck down much religion; prayers are no longer heard in the schools and atheism reigns instead. Churches have declined in spirit and few Americans really pray anymore.

How many American Christians are really ready to die for God?

WAKE UP, AMERICA!

Moon calls for a reawakening of the American Christian spirit. He calls for a pilgrim spirit to carry on the great works of the founders of this country. Individualism, he says, must be bound into a God-centered ideology.

The non-English speaking Moon, who gives his speeches through a Korean interpreter, admits that he is questioned as to how he can be a spokesman for America. But he retorts that there are too few Americans who can take the responsibility for America. We apparently need the outside help. A new spiritual nation must be created in America so God can dwell here.

Moon has come to America, he says, as part of God's will. For 6,000 years God has been working toward the building of the American nation and the entire future of the world depends on it.

"Therefore, I have come to America, where I have become one voice crying in the wilderness of the 20th century," declares the speaker, paraphrasing John the Baptist and Isaiah.

Moon has been chosen by God to be His messenger, to sound an alarm.

SALVATION—KOREAN-STYLE

Moon feels that a new movement, virtually a new religion, is needed to ignite world salvation. No longer can Christian churches be counted on to be effective; no longer can American democracy serve as the necessary force in the world today. A new ideal and new leadership is needed; "A new ideological movement is absolutely necessary."

This is to be the Moonie movement. American youth, under Moon, are pouring their energies into world salvation, the speaker says. They are the ones who will rekindle the American spirit. America's churches, business leaders and government can no longer be counted on, but her youth, under the right leadership, will prevail.

Moon says he has initiated a new American pilgrim movement. Why should a Korean initiate an American movement? Moon says that it there is no one in America to meet this great need there is no reason why an outsider cannot fulfill the duty. This is how God has worked in the past, after all, calling devout people from foreign lands. Some outsider is badly needed to come to America and stop God from leaving it! Moon says he gave up a good life and a good ministry in Korea to come to this country, and his followers were in tears when he departed. But his work now is more important and he is willing to make the sacrifice.

There is to be a "new world" begun from Moon's new pilgrim movement in America. There is no other alternative possible. That movement, that ideal world, will be undertaken by The Unification Church.

The Unification Church has an ideal, a philosophy and a method for bringing renewal to America and the world. It has the capacity to take in both the materialistic civilization of the western world and the spiritual civilization of the eastern world. The Unification Church will succeed in bringing in one unified culture in the world.

Korea is to be especially honored in Moon's new scheme of things. Moon feels that it is God's will that Korea be the ignition point of His final dispensation for the entire world. Korea is "the final bastion of the free world in Asia," and serves as a joining point of East and West, so it must be safeguarded and preserved.

The coming world of "unity, harmony and peace," will issue forth from Korea, according to Rev. Moon.

BOOS FOR THE FUEHRER

All of the foregoing represents Moon's American philosophy, on which he lectures under various titles— "God's Plan for America," "God's Hope for America." The basic message is varied for the particular audience, the biblical stress being apparent in my own initiation lecture, and the patriotic aspect being brought out strongly for general audiences.

Moon has given this message a number of times publicly, and notably in the House Caucus Room to members of the

U. S. Congress, Dec. 18, 1975. He also gave it in Washington at a public auditorium Oct. 21, 1973.

The most effective occasion for this American speech was Moon's Bicentennial God Bless America Festival, at Yankee Stadium, June 1, 1976, where the message fell in well with the bicentennial celebrations throughout the land. Moon, expert at gathering public notice, capitalized on the moment, expecting a gigantic crowd and complete acceptance.

But Yankee Stadium turned out to be a great disappointment for the Moonies. They were annoyed by picketers, plastered by the media, including Time, the Wall Street Journal, and The National Observer, and they gathered far fewer fans than they expected.

The Journal was particularly unmerciful. In an article called, "Rev. Moon Strikes Out at the Stadium,"* writer Benjamin Stein said, "If you are worried about the Reverend Sun Myung Moon, you can stop right now. Based on his Tuesday night performance at the Yankee Stadium . . . his charisma and attraction are somewhat less than Wayne Hays'. His extravaganza was an exercise in how not to influence people."

Stein told of being offered free tickets many times on New York streets by non-English speaking Moonies, but "An organization that has Korean-speaking people trying to preach on the streets of New York City is not what you call a public relations heavyweight."

The writer described the program, featuring the "New York City Symphony": "Interestingly enough, most of its members were Oriental. I later learned that they are the Rev. Moon's traveling accompanists, who had simply been called The New York City Symphony for this occasion. Once

* The Wall Street Journal, Thurs., June 3, 1976

again, it was not exactly an overpowering psychological coup.''

The Moonies did not do especially well trying to witness to the crowd of mostly youngsters: ''Whenever one of the Moon acolytes came around, wearing a crazed smile, as they all do, the kids near me smiled too and pushed and shoved the Moonie until he retreated, clutching his flyers.''

The master himself was not well received: ''The appearance of Rev. Moon ignited an immense chorus of booing and catcalling from the area around me. Kids threw everything in sight—firecrackers, soda bottles and cans, and crumpled up flyers for Rev. Moon. Again, not quite the reception you would expect for a likely Fuehrer.''

Stein was distinctly unimpressed by all that he saw at the stadium, and he analyzed Moon and his movement in an editorial passage:

> I don't know why people become Moonies. The movement is not hypnotic or fascinating, at least to me. In fact, neither the Rev. Moon nor his followers have any saving grace whatsoever. I have the feeling that the kids who become caught up in the Unification Church could get caught up in anything, and that whatever anguish they cause their parents, they are no threat to society. If the God Bless America Rally at Yankee Stadium was any indication of what the Rev. Moon is, there is one good word for him—pitiful.

MOON THE MESSIAH?

The National Observer also panned the Yankee Stadium rally, and flatly termed Moon the Lord of the Second Advent, in Moonie parlance.* Writer Michael Putney

* *National Observer,* June 12, 1976

described the Moonies; "First you notice their clothes. They look flash-frozen out of the 50's, as if the anti-war marches and the civil-rights sit-ins of the 60's never happened. The boys have white-sidewall haircuts and wear conservative suits and ties. The girls wear modest dresses and no make-up.

"Then you notice their smiles—open, warm, affectionate and non-stop. When they speak of their leader, their smiles widen and become almost beatific, ethereal, otherworldly. They seem totally without guile, but beneath the smiles—less childlike than childish—is something slightly supercilious, slightly secretive, that seems to say, 'I know something that you don't.'

"And they do. They 'know' that Sun Myung Moon is the Lord of the Second Advent, the Third Adam, the new Messiah."

Putney characterized the movement accurately as a quasi-family. "They are his disciples—Moonies to the uninitiated, the Family among themselves, and obedient children to the man they call Master. It is very definitely one man's family."

The Moonies think they have an important mission: "They all believe that Moon, a 56-year old self-ordained Korean evangelist, has been chosen to fulfill Christ's mission on earth. That mission, Moon repeatedly teaches in his lectures and in *Divine Principle*, his bible, was to marry and father children whose blood was not tainted by Satan. His followers believe that Moon, who lives in a sumptuous $625,000 estate near Tarrytown, N.Y., with his fourth wife and eight children, is succeeding where Jesus failed."

The periodicals disagree on how many wives Moon has had in his time. This fact, like the details of his training and ordination, is hard to come by. In any case, whatever wife he has at any given time is apparently one of the world's two True Parents, according to his doctrine.

Putney quotes a Moonie booklet about Moon's Easter, 1936 interview with Jesus: "Jesus explained God's desire to establish His Kingdom on earth and presented the need for someone on earth to take up this mission. He asked Reverend Moon to assume this responsibility."

Putney interviewed some angry parents, and a set of satisfied parents, too. One mother of a Moonie told him, "I believe that it is a political movement and one that poses a grave threat to our country." She pointed to Moon's friendly relations with the dictatorial regime of President Park of South Korea, as well as Moonie lobbying on Capitol Hill. She said, "He himself says he will 'conquer and subjugate the world' and I think he believes it. I don't think Moon lies. He's just so outlandishly truthful that nobody disbelieves him."

A Rabbi disclosed to Putney that he is scared of Moon. A leader in the anti-Moon group, Citizens Engaged in Reuniting Families, the Rabbi had testified to a congressional hearing in Washington, February, 1976: "The last time I witnessed a movement that had these characteristics—a single authoritarian head, fanatical followers, absolute unlimited funds, hatred for everyone on the outside, suspicion against their parents—was the Nazi Youth movement. And I tell you, I'm scared."

The set of satisfied parents said about Moon, "We're behind him 100%. They're a great bunch of kids. I know there's been a lot of adverse publicity about parents being excluded, but that's not true with us . . . What can be wrong if they believe in God? What could be wrong with that?"

The sidewalk outside Yankee Stadium was described by Putney as "An Alice's Restaurant of religion—you can get anything you want. Orthodox Jews search for Jewish Moonies; Baptists search for anyone. Lutherans pamphleteer courteously, the Jesus People agressively. A band of 30 chanting Hare Krishna people sweep up the sidewalk to the beat of drums and the tinkle of bells . . .''

That religious circus of protestors looking for their own contained a number of placards which Putney found interesting: ''Come see Moon's Unification Robots. They walk! They smile! Wind them up and out comes the Master's voice.'' The Moonies countered with a poster of their own: ''God's love conquers nastiness.''

Behind the scenes, Moon is getting some official scrutiny, the article revealed. The large amount of property Moon controls enjoys tax-exempt status as a church and the protection of the first amendment, but ''Rep. Peter Peyser of New York confirmed last week that the Internal Revenue Service is looking into the Unification Church and its dozens of affiliated organizations. And Rep. Elizabeth Holtzman of Brooklyn revealed that she has asked the U. S. Immigration and Naturalization Service some pointed questions about Moon, who was granted a permanent visa in 1973.''

The article went on to describe the Stadium event in much the same terms as the Wall Street Journal article, with writer Putney being distinctly unimpressed.

(It may well be the scrutiny of government organizations that caused the mysterious announcement July 29, 1976, that Moon may possibly leave this country.* The Church will go on as usual but Moon may choose to have his headquarters elsewhere.)

A picket sign photographed by Time bore the message, ''PARENTS BEWARE. MOON WANTS YOUR CHILDREN.'' The Flag Day Time article characterized Moon as

---

* *Dallas Morning News*, July 29, 1976 (writer: Carolyn Raeke, Washington)

"that sleek, self-anointed savior from Korea." Rev. Moon had anticipated some very big things at the stadium—"He had forecast an overflow crowd of 200,000, perhaps an absurd million, for his stadium extravaganza"* but the 54,000-seat stadium was about half filled.

The Moonies had put their all into this bicentennial effort, even putting on a show of street-cleaning in New York, singing and public good cheer, but the crusty New Yorkers, veterans of every sort of pitchmen, largely rejected the theatrics. The New York Times** ran the text of Moon's keynote address, but The Times gave no quarter: "The Unification Church is only one of dozens of religious cults that are drawing young Americans these days. Other notable ones are Hare Krishna, the Children of God, Brother Julius, Love Israel and the Divine Light Mission."

The article went on, though, to give Moon special credit for his non-spiritual talents: "But Moon's penchant for publicity and totalitarian trappings attracts the most attention and stirs the strongest emotions." Truly, Moon's sweeping promises of unifying the world, his unabashed Americanism and, particularly, his clever identification with Christianity and the Bible have made the Moonies stand out among cults in this country despite their relatively small numbers. It is hard to picture, say, the Hare Krishna folks getting the attention of the U. S. Congress.

"GOD'S HOPE FOR AMERICA"

Moon's bicentennial message, this time called "God's Hope for America," was a pre-softened, tenderized version of his basic American philosophy. Gone were all references

* Reprinted by permission from *Time*, The Weekly Newsmagazine;
** copyright *Time Inc.*

to Abraham and the other biblical personalities whose failures made Moon's present work necessary. And gone, in highly Jewish New York City, was God's rejection of Israel as the chosen nation. Moon stuck to looking at the greatness of America and the unified-world possibilities for the future.

"God seeks to build one family of man," Moon taught in the stadium.* "True Americans are those who have a universal mind. True Americans are those who believe in the one family of man, transcendent of color and nationality as willed by God. True Americans are those who are proud of such international families, churches and of the nation which consists of all peoples."

And as to why America needs Rev. Moon: "Ladies and gentlemen, if there is illness in your home, do you not need a doctor from outside? If your home catches on fire do you not need firefighters from outside? God has sent me to America in the role of a doctor, in the role of a firefighter. That is why I have come to America."

Moon dealt briefly with some of the rejection he gets among Americans who find his methods distasteful: "Good medicine may taste bitter, and an operation may involve some pain, but the treatment must begin at once. Should a patient complain and push away the doctor's hand when he touches the infected part?

Truly, America owes this selfless doctor a great deal, to hear him tell it: "For the last three years, with my entire heart and soul I have been teaching American youth a new revelation from God . . . Your dedicated sons and daughters are champions of God crusading for the victory of God's will . . . It is our mission to build the Kingdom of God right here on earth."

---

* All direct quotes from his speech as reprinted in the *New York Times*, June 3, 1976.

The theme of world unification was restated in many forms for the Yankee stadium crowd, and even compared to the American Fore Fathers' building of "One Nation Under God." We are now to go forward to build "One *World* Under God!"

"To do this," preached Moon, "Christianity of the world must unite. The church must liberate herself from sectarianism. She must undergo a drastic reform, and achieve an ecumenical and an inter-religious unity. For this we need a spiritual revolution. We need a new ideology, and this new ideology must incorporate Oriental philosophy, uniting the cultures of the East and the West."

Going on with his personal one-world philosophy, Moon explained where his movement comes in: "This new ideology will also be capable of unifying all the existing religions and ideologies of the world. Therefore it has come in the form of a new religious or spiritual movement. The Unification Church Movement has been created by God to fulfill that mission."

When America has been reawakened, according to Rev. Moon, "the rest of the world will follow America's example and will build the Kingdom of God upon their respective lands. Then we shall all truly become brothers and sisters under one Father, God. This will be a world of love, a world of happiness. Our planet will be one home, and mankind will be one family . . . Indeed, it will be the Kingdom of God on earth. We will build it with our hands."

THE BIBLE TELLS US SO

For those of us familiar with the Bible and with end times prophecy Rev. Moon certainly strikes some familiar chords. In fact, he is a broadside target.

But it must be kept in mind that this sort of teaching, attractive and appealing, is meant for those who do not know the scriptures. Without the Biblical warnings concerning this very kind of end times message—one unified world, one religious system, men bringing in the Kingdom with their own hands, the denigration of Israel, a new Messiah—we might all fall prey. How luxurious it is to dream of a world such as the one Moon pictures for us. How tempting it is to follow him anywhere, if he can only lead us to it.

"Many will come in my name," lamented the Lord, deceiving even "the very elect" as the end times come upon the world. "But those who endure to the end will be saved" (Mt. 24).

Refuting Moon on biblical grounds is very easy, but it must be realized that the vast majority of this country and the world haven't the vaguest notion of what he is really up to, or what the Bible says about it. Most of those who follow Moon do so for the best of what they consider spiritual reasons. They believe that Rev. Moon, the Kingdom-maker, is truly sent by God.

Refutations of Moon's American theology will be saved for the final chapter. First, we should consult this remarkable "savior" further. He has a great deal to say about Jesus and about a completely different personality, the coming Messiah.

Chapter Four

Moon On Jesus

Moon on Jesus

Moon just doesn't see Jesus in the same way Christians do. Jesus' mission just didn't work out, according to Rev. Moon.

Moon has talked to God, Jesus and John the Baptist, and he, Moon, has discovered what went wrong in the gospel days. God has seen fit to reveal some amazing truths to Moon, and Moon is willing to reveal these to the world at this time.

And this is a fitting time for such revelations. God and Rev. Moon are about to change the world, according to Moon.

And now Moon has a difficult task; he has to tell the people at large the secrets of the Bible which he has learned and the people are not likely to believe him, he feels. After all, who believed Noah, he laments, or Abraham, in their times? Or, most regrettably, who believed John the Baptist, or Jesus Himself?

Jesus' failure is placed squarely on the people who insisted to take the scriptures literally and failed to perceive the first Messiah's true purposes. He was a laborer, a carpenter, and the people were expecting something else as their Savior. He was an illegitimate child and this caused great trauma in His own family.

Moon pictures Joseph as unable to appreciate that his betrothed, Mary, had conceived a child by God. He teaches that Joseph was greatly injured by Mary's apparent unfaithfulness. "My wife is not truly honest with me," Moon "quotes" Joseph, and so Jesus was off to a bad start. Further evidence of the emotional upheaval in the Messiah's own family comes at the wedding at Cana (Jn. 2), in which Jesus refers to his mother as "Woman" rather than "mother". Moon feels that this passage indicates the difficult relationship Jesus had with His own kin, and if He was unaccepted at home how much more would He be spurned by the public?

Moon feels that the Bible's very brief record of Jesus' initial 30 years before His public ministry indicates that it was not a glorious one. The Messiah must have lived in "sorrow and grief" before He stated "I am the way, the truth and the life." People were therefore astonished when He came forward as their Deliverer.

Moon feels that many of the religious people today would have great difficulty accepting Jesus, given His personal circumstances and low position. Jesus confused the people; he sounded so strange, so outrageous. "Even John the Baptist had difficulty seeing Jesus as the Son of God, and John was supposed to come to prepare the people and make straight the way of the Lord."

Today we can accept Jesus much more easily, with hindsight. But back then He was hard to believe. He was truly the Son of God, but people just could not see Him that way. If we of today had lived back then we might have even compounded their ignorance, feels Moon. We must not make the mistake of failing to receive the Messiah again.

The society Jesus chose to mix with—harlots, tax collectors, fishermen—did not help His ministry much. The people objected to that side of Him as well, and so would we, feels Moon. The Savior was utterly misunderstood.

The folks who took the scriptures literally expected to see Elijah the prophet announcing Jesus, but he didn't show up at all. If only the people had realized that the Bible is to be understood *symbolically* they would have understood that John was an adequate announcer of Jesus. This situation presented quite a problem to Jesus.

John the Baptist was sent, of course, in the spirit of Elijah as the prophet of Jesus. But John himself failed in his faith and doubted Jesus. John eventually deserted Jesus, according to Rev. Moon, and this wrought much damage to the credibility and ministry of the Messiah. It was also most disappointing to God; His sought-after love relationship ideal was foiled by John's lack of faith.

Again, with the prophet Daniel, the scriptures were interpreted far too literally. Daniel said, "I saw in the night visions, and behold, with the clouds of heaven there came one like the son of a man," according to Moon (this closely paraphrases Dan. 7:13, with some essentials left out). So apparently the literal interpreters expected the Messiah from the clouds and Jesus failed to fulfill that.

As to this being prophecy for the Second Coming of Christ, Moon believes that no such interpretation is possible. All the prophets were consummated in John the Baptist and all prophecy prior to him was to be fulfilled in the time of Jesus. There is no prophecy in the Old Testament that applies to the future, according to Moon.

It is the truth that will set us free, however difficult the truth is to accept. Jesus was a man, the incarnate of God in the flesh. If Jesus had not been crucified by misunderstanding people he would have certainly brought the Kingdom of Heaven right then and there.

But the cross ruined all of God's plans.

The cross was a horrible, heinous mistake. Ignorant

people crucified Jesus Christ, says Moon, and spoiled God's 4,000 years of labor toward Jesus' coming.

God certainly did not work all that time in the preparation of His chosen people and nation to have it all end in ignominious execution of the would-be Savior. God did not so carefully lay the foundation for the coming of the Messiah only to have it foiled by the stupidity of men. The cross apparently surprised and disappointed God, and new plans had to be undertaken.

If Jesus came today, speculates Moon at this point, would Christians nail Him to a cross? Would that be His glory, his mission, his destiny today? No! We must not do that. We must correct the mistakes of the past. God's former chosen people had a choice between a Kingdom and a cross and they chose the cross. We must choose the Kingdom today.

Moon teaches carefully Israel's rejection of the Messiah. "He came to his own home, and his own people received him not," he paraphrases John 1:11. "None of the rulers of this age understood this; for if they had they would not have crucified the Lord of Glory," he renders 1 Cor. 2:8. (Moon's paraphrases, to be fair to him, are given originally in Korean, interpreted on the spot into English and finally edited for publication. He is by and large accurate in his renditions of scripture. Open to more question are his applications of the scriptures he cites.)

If the teachers of Judaism had not been "slaves" (Moon's word) to the literal interpretations of the scriptures they would have realized who Jesus really was and we would have had the Kingdom a long time ago. But it is now time to repair the damage. The truth of Jesus' mission is now revealed.

Christians will not repeat the Jewish mistake, says Moon. Understanding as we now do what men failed to grasp in the gospel times, we can now bring on the Kingdom at will.

The time of the Second Advent is at hand, according to Moon (in the following chapter we will take up Moon's unique idea of the Second Advent).

The foundation of Christianity is the cross, and this, to Moon, is an awful mistake. It is a mistaken belief. Both God and Christ are sadly misunderstood as matters now stand in the world.

But help is now here! God chose a 16 year-old youth on Easter Morning in 1936 on a Korean mountainside, and this youth, Sun Myung Moon, will bring the truth to the world. Moon interviewed God and Jesus that Easter, and the whole of God's plan for men was revealed to him.

WHAT GOD TOLD MOON

God is to be pitied, according to Moon's interview with Him. He is isolated and has lost His children.

Jesus was to liberate God from His isolation by starting the Kingdom of God on the earth, but without the cooperation of the chosen people (of the time) Jesus could not do that. God could only expect, after the Jews rejected Jesus, a minimal accomplishment of His original plan.

The problems with Jesus' mission developed very early, according to what God told Moon. The three wise men who attended Christ in the manger did not fulfill their task, which was actually to raise Jesus until the day of His marriage. They would have been His first three disciples, and John the Baptist would have been His fourth. Instead, Jesus had to look for new disciples.

John's failure toward Jesus is especially reprehensible. John was well educated, according to Moon, and "highly esteemed;" John was "recognized as a great prophet" while Jesus was unscholarly. Because of their obvious differences John did not dream that Jesus was to become the Savior.

As to Jesus' marriage, He was to father a new race of believers. Since Adam and Eve fell, God needed a new couple on earth from which would descend His believing people. But Jesus was unable to find His bride because of the rejection of the people. The King was supposed to have a Queen, but under the circumstances this couldn't be accomplished. The True Parents of mankind should have come in the time of Jesus, but obviously that was made impossible.

If only Jesus had married there would have issued forth a new nation of faithful people, and they would have been able to provide salvation for all of mankind. Mankind needs new True Parents. Jesus should have married a ''restored Eve'' and gone on to produce a race of sinless children on the earth. They would have saved all men.

In the manner of the Garden of Eden, though, God's plans were thwarted by disobedience and rebellion, and the Kingdom could not be established and God remained in isolation. Instead of the King of Israel (Jesus) establishing a real Kingdom of God on earth, which would have restored all of God's children to Him, the plan was defeated. God had to allow His Son to be sacrificed.

Now the cross was a victory of a kind for God, according to Moon's revelations. Jesus was resurrected and this brought Christianity a spiritual victory. God could now claim the souls of men, in exchange for their bodies.

Where we stand now, after Jesus' resurrection, is that salvation for our *souls* is available through belief in Christ, but our bodies remain in the province of Satan. God ransomed His son in order to win a partial victory; He at least provided for the redemption of the souls of those who accept Jesus. But the *bodies* of Christians remain unpure and sinful, and so more help is needed.

The Lord of the Second Advent will finish the job, according to Moon. This will not be Jesus, again, but a man imbued with the Spirit of Christ. And he will be able to provide not only spiritual salvation for those who need it, but also the redemption of the body. People will be *totally* purified at the coming of the new Messiah.

It has been God's desire throughout man's long history to locate a man who would truly love Him, and to have that man be accepted among the people of the world. Jesus truly loved God but of course He was not accepted. Now there have been many people willing to *receive* God's love but no one other than Jesus, so far, willing to *love God*. God has been set aside, betrayed, even by His very saints. Spiritually weak people are all around today, taking in God's blessings but remaining unwilling to love God back. Christians are spiritually impotent, unable to really love God.

And so God remains alone, unloved and truly isolated from His children. Truly He is to be pitied, Moon says.

But fortunately, Rev. Moon loves God! In his speech, Rev. Moon assures God that all is not lost:

> I would tell him not to worry about anything. I am in His place to work for Him until the last one of all humanity has been turned back to Him. I feel that I am responsible for the totalization of all the betrayals committed by past humanity and all those saints who failed in their missions. Thus, I have to return glory to God, to clear away His resentment and sorrow and disillusionment.

MAN'S CHOICE

Rev. Moon has made the right choice where God is concerned, to take him at his word. All other men must also make a choice, as to their own love of God. Moon teaches that God set up this choice after the Garden of Eden and the fall, having few delusions about the behavior of His earthly children. He allowed two opposed prophecies to exist side by side, since man is so changeable, alternating between good and evil:

> For unto us a child is born, a son is given; and the government will be upon his shoulder . . . (Isa. 9:6 . . .)

> Surely he has born our griefs and carried our sorrows: yet we esteem him stricken, smitten by God and afflicted. But he was wounded for our transgressions, he was bruised for our iniquities; upon him was the chastisement that made us whole; and with his stripes we are healed. (Isa. 53:4-5)

The same prophet seemed to see two different destinies for the Messiah. The first prophecy, which contains the Messiah's titles as the ruler of the coming Kingdom, was to be effected *if* Israel received her Messiah. The second prophecy, the one which actually occurred, was to show what would happen if Israel rejected the Messiah.

It was not the will of God, teaches Moon, for Jesus to die on the cross. If it were, Judas would be a hero, having helped Jesus accomplish his work. If Jesus were supposed to have died He would never have shouted from the cross, ''My God, my God, Why hast thou forsaken me?'' Instead He would have cried, ''God I am honored! Rejoice, Father, I am victorious!''

No, Jesus was crucified by the faithlessness of man, in opposition to God's will. Men failed again; they made the wrong choice. They killed God's best effort to reconcile with His children. They prevented the marriage of Jesus Christ and a new Eve and thus they eliminated the possibility of the new race of sinless human beings.

But the Lord of the Second Advent will succeed. The Christians will be more accepting than the Jews were. "He is coming as a man" and he will judge the world. From out of the waters of mankind, the presently unpure and tainted seas of people, he will come to purify men and unite with them to establish the successful Eden.

MOON—THE LAST HOPE FOR MANKIND

All of the above theology was gleaned from two of Rev. Moon's speeches, "God's Way of Life," and "The New Future of Christianity," which he gave on Sept. 17 and 18, 1974. He gave the first at the Waldorf Astoria Hotel for an audience of 1,700 and the second at Madison Square Garden for a full-house plus thousands in the streets, according to the New York Times, Sept. 19, 1974.

The Madison Square Garden evening was a success, coming early in Moon's New York City ministry. "The young, the old, blacks, whites, the middle-aged—they all came to hear the preacher, and like some of them told me, they came to be reborn."* The Moonies were their usual community-minded selves, cleaning the streets and taking away their advertising posters in an all-night session following the Garden program, the Times specified on Sept. 20, 1974.

The advertising circulars carried a picture of Moon and the message "Last Hope for Mankind . . . The Messiah."

* *Newsbeat,* Sept. 24, 1974

WHERE TO BEGIN?

It is hard to know where to begin to refute Moon's ideas about Jesus. He brings us entirely new ideas taken from his reported interviews with God, Jesus, and John the Baptist, and his philosophy stands outside the scriptures in many cases. Even where he quotes scripture his interpretations are entirely new.

The idea of a new revelation or a personal interview with God for the founder of a cult is of course not a very new idea. Joseph Smith, the original Latter Day Saint, found new information from God to start his Mormon church; Ellen Gould White enjoyed some 2,000 visions through which she initiated and guided the Seventh Day Adventists; and lately, folks say they are getting information from UFO's, the spirit world, Hindu deities and gurus, and everything else under, and over the sun. A personal interview with God, et. al., is almost old hat.

Moon's technique of handling scripture comes under the general heading of *eisogesis*—reading in ideas not given in the text. Normal biblical scholarship is called *exegesis*—the explanation of ideas already contained in the text. With the former method the possibilities for developing new doctrines are virtually limitless; the Bible is a lengthy book containing many symbols.

If one comes to the scriptures with a pre-developed notion of what one wants them to say, it is possible to ''prove'' many strange concepts. Adding in a snippet of scripture here and there makes the new doctrine seem very biblical indeed.

Still and all, Moon has a number of truths scattered among his doctrines and his power as a preacher is unquestionable. He undoubtedly convinces a goodly proportion of those who give him a hearing, and have little

Bible knowledge of their own. His highly intelligent-sounding reconstructions of Jesus and the gospel bring to an already fascinating topic a completely new approach. Moon declares his messages in the terms of a real prophet and he mesmerizes his listeners.

Korean Lt. Col. Bo Hi Pak, Moon's special assistant and interpreter, characterizes Moon as a prophet, contrasting him with Billy Sunday, Dwight Moody and Billy Graham, who are or were only teachers. Moon is here to reveal *new* information from God, rather than to merely repeat what has been said before.

THE GOSPEL ACCORDING TO MOON

Getting to Moon's gospel, it amounts to one more man-centered, earthbound philosophy. In any "liberal" church, where the scriptures are taken symbolically, if read at all, one can find such unbiblical reproductions of what might have been.

There is no hint in the gospel of Joseph feeling that Mary was not honest with him. There is not the vaguest suggestion of John the Baptist not believing in Christ; we all ask the question at one time or another, "Are you He that was to come?" There is no indication that the wise men were to have any further ministry with Jesus than that which is stated. The whole notion of God trying a plan and being disappointed with its failure is odious to thinking Christians.

The idea of Jesus establishing the Kingdom back in gospel times if Israel had accepted Him has more credence. Jesus said that the Kingdom was at hand. But we really don't know this as fact because it didn't happen. To teach it dogmatically is merely an exercise of the imagination; to use an idea like this to promote a new doctrine is simple opportunism.

Israel's rejection of Jesus was partial, not complete, or we wouldn't have a Christian church at all, it would seem. Moon does not deal with the Jewish apostles who took the word of the Messiah to the world, began the first churches and acted in a manner sacrificial enough to satisfy the high-living Moon's most stringent requirements. The Messiah was Jewish, the disciples were all Jews, the Apostles were all Jews and all of the original believers were Jews. The Pharisees were astonished at the great number of Jews who received Jesus (Jn. 12:19).

The idea of God rejecting Israel because of their failures is dealt with succinctly by Paul: "Hast God cast away His people; God forbid!" (Rom. 11:1). Paul wrote this statement in his letter to the Romans, the very people who Moon thinks God switched to. Paul declared plainly, "I am an Israelite . . ." Romans 9 through 11 expresses in three chapters the hopelessness of trying to disenfranchise Israel from her chosen status. Jeremiah sums up powerfully:

> Thus saith the Lord; If heaven above can be measured, and the foundations of the earth searched out beneath, I will also cast off all the seed of Israel for all that they have done, saith the Lord. (Jer. 31:37)

People who teach new Bible interpretations frequently attack the Jews unnecessarily. God told Abraham, "I will bless them that bless thee, and curse him that curseth thee" (Gen. 12:3) but there have always been legions of unbelievers to curse the Jews. The Jews stand firmly in the world today as stunning proof of God's ongoing plan, the same plan He adopted with Abraham. Moon has apparently not appreciated the dramatic recovery of Israel in our time, or misunderstands its purpose in the fulfillment of God's original plan.

This brings up Moon's casual statement that all Old

Testament prophecy was to be fulfilled in the time of Jesus. This incredible view would throw out 50% of biblical prophecy, including a great many of Jesus' own prophecies (Mt. 24:15, e.g.), and make the complete works of the major and minor prophets meaningless. In a stroke Moon does away with all Second Advent scripture, including the rapture of the church, the tribulation period, the antichrist (whom Moon never mentions, at least intentionally), Armageddon, the return of Jesus to the earth and the particulars of the true, biblically-explained Kingdom of God. Moon's view of prophecy also pointedly throws out the recovery of Israel by the Jewish people and the large part it plays in the end times.

Instead, the scriptures have been reinterpreted by Moon to lead to his *own* coming messiah. All the condemnation of those who took the scriptures *literally* in the past seems aimed at keeping people today from examining the Bible too closely. Obviously even a cursory reading of scripture would expose Moon's doctrines for what they really are.

Jesus' marriage is almost too revolting a doctrine to even deal with, but it should be recognized that this absurdity serves a definite purpose in Moon's scheme of things. We recall Cynthia Slaughter bowing to Moon's picture and being made to call Moon and his present wife ''True Parents.'' If Moon can get people believing that it is a *married couple* with which God wants to start the Kingdom, he can cut his wife in on his future plans. We assume Rev. Moon has matured away from his reported earlier doctrine about purifying other peoples' wives, * but we can suspect that his own marriage has a great deal to do with this unjustifiable and far-flung Kingdom philosophy. Perhaps Moon and his wife, are somehow going to beget that sinless

---

* Reprinted by permission from *Time,* The Weekly Newsmagazine; copyright *Time Inc.*

race which will sanctify us all. The mind boggles!

The whole concept of human beings bringing in the Kingdom of God in their own strength is at odds with scripture. God will bring the Kingdom, Jesus will rule it, and nothing is plainer than that in scripture. Moon is right when he observes that men have never been able to accomplish God's will or achieve anything like the Kingdom on earth. But we wonder at his confidence that men inspired by Rev. Moon will be able to do what men never have done in the past.

Moon sometimes traps himself, as will happen to those who try to restate the scriptures to their own purpose. He has done away with end times prophecy as irrelevant to his doctrines, but then he must borrow on it to support some of them. Jesus' spiritual marriage to come, with the church—the Bride of Christ in scripture— is of course a Second Advent matter, explained in Rev. 19:7-8, but Moon needs it in order to have some glimmer of credence for his arcane Adam-and-Eve view of the Kingdom. Malachi's announcement of the Messiah ''before the great and dreadful day of the Lord'' (Mal. 4:5) just won't fit into the First Advent, being plainly an end times event, so Moon uses it as an example of a too-literal reading of scripture. Borrowing on Daniel 7:13, again a clear Second Advent prophecy in language and context, was equally unconvincing. It plainly showéd the return of Christ in the end times. We must marvel that anyone who disbelieves Second Advent prophecy would even open the Book of Daniel.

Another familiar strain in false doctrines is the splitting of the Christian church into good believers and not-so-good believers. Moon thinks in terms of part of each person being saved—the spiritual part—and then virtually nobody living up to true standards of loving God. This sort of doctrine worries people, even believing people ("For there shall arise false Christs, and false prophets . . . insomuch that, if it were possible, they shall deceive the very elect," said Jesus in Matt. 24:24). People who truly want to do God's will sometimes wonder if they are succeeding. Moon plays upon this very human foible to good effect.

When Moon makes his own statements about his love for God we cannot help be impressed, if only by the oratory. How self-sacrificing he is, and how divinely inspired. He can even assure God that He has nothing to worry about; Rev. Moon is taking care of everything. Moon pities God, and goes right to the side of our stricken Father in Heaven. He is even willing to lead the rest of us doubters, if only we'll listen to him.

Moon says he feels responsible for all the misdeeds of the failing saints of the past. This technique makes the hearts of the audience go out to him in his humility and long-suffering, but it bears an unkindness to legions of truly self-sacrificing Christians who have loved God, done His will and kept the Christian faith burning brightly for centuries throughout the world. The armies of missionaries, the unsung heroes who restore the most forgotten of human creatures to their God, the plain church people the world around, must get just a modicum of credit for loving the Lord and pursuing His will. This fatuous latter day "prophet" in his $625,000 mansion overlooking the Hudson, supported by endless armies of panhandlers, is hardly the judge of world Christianity.

MOON'S NEW FUTURE OF CHRISTIANITY

Moon's concept of men having a choice as to whether to follow God or not is quite true to scripture, but the manner in which he illustrates and utilizes the concept is very suspect. True, Isaiah gave two differing pictures of the Messiah—as King and as suffering servant. Jesus has accomplished His sacrifical mission on behalf of the world and is to return as King. Few Christians question that.

But Moon, remember, has done away with the return of Christ and all prophecy pertaining to the Second Advent, and so he is stuck with two different prophecies to be fulfilled in one coming. His solution to this dilemma is to come up with a sort of "either-or" arrangement, where God proposed two possible plans for the Messiah and then sat back to see which one men would choose.

Disappointed, God saw men choose the suffering servant prophecy, and so Jesus never became King, in Moon's system. Therefore, we have prophecy that can never be fulfilled and is nullified. Jesus is not coming back—some other man will be the new Messiah—and so part of Isaiah has now become void.

But Isaiah wrote *God's* Word. Even Moon agrees that God is the true author of scripture. So we come to an even bigger dilemma—God has said some things which no longer pertain; men have made some of God's prophecies nonsense.

Now we must begin taking pages out of the Bible, if we are to understand things Moon's way.

We are back to a simple problem that crops up with every "symbolic" rendition of scripture—some part of the Bible won't work and has to be skipped for the sake of the system. Likewise with Jesus' words from the cross; Moon has selected "Why hast thou forsaken me?" (as Jesus took our place) and left out, "Father, forgive them," and "It is finished" (or, "Paid in full," a more accurate translation of the Greek expression).

The resurrection more plainly shows Jesus' victory, but

doesn't fit especially well in Moon's system, and so the cross becomes a *partial* triumph for God. Now we are saved spiritually but not physically, and we need additional help that Jesus couldn't provide. Jesus isn't coming back, notwithstanding that he stated, "I go to prepare a place for you . . . I will come again and receive you unto myself . . ." (Jn. 14:2-3).

Things get so complicated when we define our religion first and then try to justify it from God's Word.

As to Moon's New Future of Christianity, not very many Christians think we need one. The future announced in the Bible seems satisfactory to believers and it is difficult to picture any improvement. God's plan has its difficulties for some, but it *is* God's plan, and it has proved very acceptable to those who believe in God.

Nevertheless, Moon has a new future for Christianity and it all revolves around the coming Messiah. Let us look now at his remarkable "Lord of the Second Advent."

Chapter Five

The Future, According To Moon

The Future,
According to Moon

As the prophet of God for our time, Rev. Moon has revealed that God needs help. He, God, must find some person in every age to be His instrument and to spread His word.

The Almighty is handicapped because men don't love Him, and He is unable to act to bring in the Kingdom of God without the help of faithful men, according to Moon.

"Surely the Lord God does nothing without revealing his secret to his servants the prophets," Moon paraphrases Amos 3:7, but happily Moon is here with us and we can know what God wants to do and where He needs our help.

Moon has been called by God, Moon says, and the Korean has obliged God by agreeing to help Him. Angels will aid the man who reassures God about His plans and offers help to Him, and in this way men can control their own destiny. Since angels must be helping Moon, he is very successful. The rest of us can be successful, too, if we will help God with His plans. We can bring in the Kingdom and we can assure ourselves of a bright future, if only we will be God's instruments along with Rev. Moon.

"He who has ears to hear, let him hear," Moon appeals, in the words of the Lord (Luke 14:35). By loving God, we can control God and His plans to our betterment. And God wants these good things for all of us, of course.

Moon has stepped out and told God that he will take the

responsibility for this present age and bring in the Kingdom now. This is the nature of God's true children, preaches Moon, to offer their help to God and to work ceaselessly toward the Kingdom.

If we give God enough help in this project, then God will be able to establish the Lord of the Second Advent, the coming Messiah, and through him restore his original design of creation.

But it should be understood, Moon says, that God cannot establish His Kingdom without our help. We must all pitch in for our lonely Father in heaven who has seen failure time and again among His children. Our omnipotent God is dependent on us for our aid.

The many religions now established all fall short of really helping the Almighty, Moon thinks, and a new ideology is again called for. If the Lord of the Second Advent is to make a successful appearance, men must dig in and prepare a place for him. None of our religions are in complete accord with God's will today, but there is a new spiritual age coming in which believing men will truly triumph.

Faith and reality will unite in this coming age. Our spiritual faith will be realized in a physical world, and spiritual phenomena—miracles—will be commonplace on earth when we bring in the Kingdom.

But each man must now be at his post, ready to assist God in this great endeavor. Particularly, the members of the Unification Church, who are leading the way, must be ready and willing to greet the Lord of the Second Advent.

WHEN THE MOONIES COME MARCHING IN

Moon says that God will succeed in this coming new effort to establish the Kingdom. He tried in Eden, he tried in

Israel, and the third time will be the charm. The number three is symbolic of perfection, says Moon, and the Kingdom of God will be established on earth on the third try.

Each of you, Moon preached to the assembled members of the Unification Church, are the beginning of the Kingdom of God. You were chosen for that purpose. As you unite in marriage and establish God-centered families you will bring forth children. Through your children you will be members of His Kingdom.

Jesus will return as a man. [It is very hard to understand what Moon means by "Jesus will return as a man." This particular speech was given to a Moonie audience, and it differs on this point from what I myself was told at Moonie headquarters. It differs from what was taught in my initiation lecture, and it differs from the statements of Moon in other contexts. Moon may mean that Jesus will return "symbolically." But on other occasions (the National Observer article, e.g.) people have been told that Moon himself is the coming Messiah. It is difficult to see how Moon can say that *Jesus* will return when he also says that the coming Messiah was born just after World War I. Also, Moon has stated that the Lord coming "on the clouds" referred to the fact that the Lord will come from among the people, and he cited Rev. 17:15 to show that clouds, or water, represented people.

Moon believes in the resurrection of Jesus, but yet he says the new Messiah will come out of today's earthly people, being born among them. Apparently Moon believes that Jesus went to heaven, but now he says that He will return from earth—or more exactly, that He is on the earth now, somewhere. God's Son was apparently born over again in the 20th century.

The best answer may be that this preacher says what he

thinks will work best, given the particular audience. To try a little of Moon's symbolic theology we might observe that the Moon goes through different phases on different evenings.]

In any case, Moon said that Jesus would come back as a man, on this occasion, and He would now be the ''Third Adam.''

''ADAM, WHERE ART THOU?''

It will be up to this Third Adam—Jesus, Moon, the ''Lord of the Second Advent,'' or whoever he turns out to be—to get married and start having children. This is what Moon says Jesus failed to do (because of the unbelief around Him).

He is to take a bride, now called the ''Perfected Eve,'' and re-create God's original ideal, the perfect Garden of Eden. This new start will bring forth sinless children and so the new Adam and Eve will be the True Parents of the coming Kingdom world. (But Moon allows worship of himself and his wife as True Parents, as we saw. Maybe Moon regards *himself* as symbolic.)

The whole idea for now is that the Moonies are to bring forth children who will later on marry the children of the new Adam and Eve, and so sinless children will come forth and repopulate the earth with believers. It is your destiny, Moon told the assembled disciples, to establish a new race, a new people for the Kingdom of God on earth.

The new Adam, Moon stresses is not coming from heaven. The Christians, he teaches, believe in a ''Rapture'' of the church, and that Jesus will lift them up to heaven. But the coming Kingdom is to be on earth. God lost His Kingdom on earth and He will reclaim His Kingdom on earth. Jesus prayed, after all, ''Thy will be done on earth as it is in heaven." Even New York City will be a part of the coming Kingdom, Moon exults.

Repeatedly Moon assures his listeners that he indeed is sent by God with a mission. In the Madison Square Garden program, where he publicly presented some of the ideas included in this chapter, he claimed to be sent in accordance with Acts 2:17: "And in the last days it shall be, that I will pour out my Spirit upon all flesh, and your sons and your daughters shall prophesy, and your young men shall see visions, and your old men shall dream dreams."

Moon says that Christians should not look upward for the coming king for He will not be there. Instead, he will come from among us, and Christians must acknowledge him. Moon says that history will repeat itself: Christians will throw stones at the new Adam and accuse him of things; they will call him a liar and a heretic. He will be persecuted by the church. (In another context Moon predicted that this would not happen—that Christians would not repeat the mistake of the Jews).

But the Christians will be very sorry when they persecute the New Adam because he will say, "Depart from me, you evil-doers."

The problem will be, again as in the first century, that the Lord of the Second Advent will come in plain flesh as a man. People will misunderstand that he is here to bring in the Kingdom and he will at first suffer and be rejected. But they will doom their own churches when they persecute the coming Messiah. They must realize, before he comes, that he is coming as a man, and not from heaven.

In any case, the New Adam will help God restore what was lost—a perfected earthly family. He will be a new ancestor for believing men because we need one. We must begin a new age with a new kind of people.

FOR JESUS' SAKE

We are nearing a new stopping and rebeginning place in the history of man, according to Moon. The Lord of the Second Advent will establish the new history of man and reveal God's new truth for the next age, just as Jesus came to end the Old Testament age with His particular truth and begin our present age.

We are to have some new truths now, or very soon. The old truths were for the old times.

Shockingly, Moon says that Jesus and His disciples cannot enter the Kingdom of Heaven until we establish it here on the earth. At present only "Paradise" is available in the Spirit world, and that is where those worthies must be at this point, awaiting our further progress. The Kingdom of heaven is prepared properly only for the new family to come, God's true children. Jesus and His disciples may enter it when it is ready.

When man's proper ancestry is established through the New Adam and his bride, then heaven on earth will be literally accomplished.

The end of our age is virtually at hand and God's new history for man is about to begin. When the Lord of the Second Advent arrives, or comes out from among us to show himself, man will have a new beginning.

Moon is particularly concerned that Christians recognize the coming new Messiah. It is as if this recognition and acceptance is Christianity's only hope. Christians *must* accept the New Adam, says Moon emphatically.

THE PROPHET COMES FIRST

Apparently the coming new Messiah will come upon us gradually. Moon stresses that no one can point to the exact day of the changes of the seasons, or the exact moment of the dawn of a new day. So it will be with the new advent. But God will not bring this day of judgment upon the world without warning; He will provide a prophet.

Moon says that God's prophet for this age must be living in the world today. He must be pure and a man of faith. He must have already demonstrated his worthiness to be chosen. As God is supreme and absolute goodness, so his prophet will be in His likeness. The prophet will be persecuted, but evildoers always persecute God's chosen ones.

(Moon refrained from claiming to be God's prophet on this occasion but declared that plainly on many others).

Moon thinks that modern Christians have things very easy. For this reason they don't tend to take God seriously and are unsanctified. They tend to walk along a path between good and evil, but this isn't satisfying to God. God's way is absolute good, and the Christians must understand that if they are to enter the new age. The coming Messiah will judge people, it should be remembered.

We need not be afraid of death in ushering in the new age. God will not forsake those who fall in His service. Jesus told us, "He who loses his life will find it." With sacrificial death for God, as a matter of fact, one reaches the very entrance to the eternal source of love.

We (members of the Unification Church) are not afraid to love, and we are not afraid of death. We are happy people, Moon assured his followers.

HERE COMES THE JUDGE

Everyone should be warned—the new Messiah is coming to judge the world.

According to the Bible, says Moon, the Lord of the Second Advent will separate the sheep from the goats.

Believers will be separated out from unbelievers in the establishment of the new Kingdom on earth. Each of us must now decide whether we will follow the Good Shepherd.

The standard of judgement, according to Moon, will be whether men have faced the truth about God as revealed by His prophet (Moon?!). Moon says God is not going to use any fire or destroy the earth, and he digresses to quite a bit of scripture on the point, but the new age *will* require men to line up with the new system and the new Messiah. New Testament truths are not important; the new Messiah will be bringing still *newer* truths, many of which are now being articulated by his prophet.

By rejection of the new truth, warns Moon, men will make themselves liable for judgment. God created the world by His Word, and the new world will be re-created by His truth. "Ye shall know the truth and the truth shall make you free," quotes Moon in the words of the gospel, but referring to this new truth that is coming. Men found death when they refused God's word. They can find life by heeding his new truth.

The prophecy of crucifixion has already been fulfilled. The prophecy of "The Lord of Glory" has yet to be accomplished. The Lord of the Second Advent will be the Lord of Glory. (Here Moon borrows upon second advent prophecy to his advantage although he said in another context that such prophecy was all fulfilled in Jesus.)

TEST THE SPIRITS

Moon counsels that we should not be listening to just anybody in these last days (praise the Lord!).

We should guard against being fooled. He goes so far as to

counsel that we should not even believe *him*, but only God. God is still available to anyone who speaks to Him, Moon says, and the truth is available to those who seek it. He says it is not a question of who is speaking but whether he is speaking the word of God. Moon is not to be believed if he is not telling God's truth, says Moon. But if Moon *is* telling the truth, it is an important and drastic truth. It is time to act on it!

We must be open to new truths, according to Moon, since God is not simply going to repeat what He has already said in the New Testament. We must be open to a new and glorious message. Moon feels that he himself is bringing much of this new truth and begs that his message be deeply considered.

THE ONE-WORLD KINGDOM

Moon gives scanty description of the coming Kingdom on earth, but one thing is sure—Korea is important in it.

Moon sees a fusion of East and West in the future Kingdom. He says that Western civilization, scientifically based, cannot be culminated without the spiritually-based Eastern civilization. These two vast cultures must fuse together with the Pacific Ocean in the middle of the new Kingdom.

The strongly anti-communist Moon does not include Russia or China in this thinking, at least not publicly, but sees the American-Korean unity as germane to the new world. A noble new civilization can be created, he feels, out of the combination of Western material progress and Eastern depth of spirituality, and this will apparently be pleasing to God.

THINGS TO COME?

The material in the above section was drawn from several of Moon's speeches which dealt with the new Messiah, variously termed also the Lord of the Second Advent, the Third Adam, and, on one occasion, Jesus.

To refute these concepts biblically becomes a little bit difficult at this point because Moon has all but departed from the Bible. Using only a scanty second advent reference here and there, he has constructed an entirely new system based on a re-created Garden of Eden situation. It is almost like arguing philosophy to refute this sort of personal-taste gospel.

But as always, the scriptures do come up, to persuade the unwary that the whole message is God's own truth, and the Bible and Christianity are consistently referred to for obvious reasons. Because Moon has introduced himself as a prophet, those who believe the real prophets should be prepared to answer him in some way, or to testify to those who might get caught up in his schemes.

The shrewd Bo Hi Pak, Moon's interpreter and general "John the Baptist", writes in his forward to Moon's book, *New Hope*, that Moon speaks in the spirit of God. The translator apologizes for the difficulties that may be experienced in reading a translation and frankly admits that Moon is difficult to translate. But the implication that God is speaking through this man is what concerns us, and what should be refuted on every occasion. We must always bear in mind that Moon normally speaks to people who haven't the vaguest idea of what God has really said in the Bible, and the Korean is masterfully persuasive in any language.

So, in the spirit of confronting Moon's truth with God's truth, we may begin with the "prophet's" concept that God cannot move without man's help.

Now this should be patently false-sounding to any man who has ever thought about God, but Moon has a clever way of putting it. That our omnipotent, universe-creating God is in need of us, is lonesome and is pitiable, is an absurdity that immediately marks out Moon for what he is. But Moon has already established the logic in the listener's mind that Jesus' mission failed. Apparently God does need help, since men crucified His Son. He needed help back then and men didn't give it to him. Moon appeals for that help now, on behalf of a troubled and ineffective God, and somehow it works. People believe it!

The idea of men controlling what God does, however, is just a misconstruction of the sovereignty of God, and little more can be said.

The strangeness of Moon's idea that Jesus is coming back and yet the New Adam, with new truths, etc., will be the new Messiah was discussed within the chapter. There can be no logic to this discrepancy except that the Master is not too clear on just *what* he thinks. Again, he may be using the good name of "Jesus" for public relations purposes ("Many will come in my name . . .")

The doctrine about the "Perfected Eve" comes out of nowhere without a breath of scriptural support. If Jesus was to get married God never mentioned it. And if Moon's coming Messiah wants to marry that's his affair, we suppose. But we cannot help but speculate who this extraordinary woman might be.

Will she be a Moonie child especially selected for this honor? Not Moon's wife, certainly? Jesus was to have married a "Restored Eve" but now we have come to a "Perfected Eve." Moon speaks of his own church members as perfected, more so than the Christians, at least, but this special calling requires quite a lady.

Perhaps Moon has a daughter who could fulfill this important role. But in any case, the plan doesn't seem very workable. Moonies are supposed to marry and have children now so that their children may intermarry with the New Adam's children to create the perfect earthly race. But it will be some time until Moonie children are grown, let alone born. The Moonies are a young group, and unless they are terrifically prolific, or unless the Lord of the Second Advent delays his coming, things aren't going to work out right.

But Moon indicates in other contexts that the New Adam is already here, born shortly after World War I. By this time he may be married and have plenty of children. That's possible.

Take Moon himself, for example. *He* was born shortly after World War I (1920) and he has eight children.

As to the Rapture of the church, Moon refutes it by saying that the Kingdom will be on earth. This represents the debate technique of putting words into the opponent's mouth. Christians do hold that the Kingdom will be established on the earth, after the Rapture. But again, Moon's listeners are probably not very knowledgeable on what Christians believe.

Moon's use of Acts 2:17, where Peter explains the appearance of the Holy Spirit at Pentecost, is a breathtaking example of quoting out of context (and how effective it can be). This scripture was used for the wrong age, to explain the wrong coming, by the wrong man, heralding the wrong messiah. This must set a new record for weird exegesis.

It is this low level of Bible understanding that makes Christians think that Moon is either truly ignorant of God's Word, or very well aware of his mistakes and working toward something very different than spiritual renewal for the world. It is curious too, in this context, that Moon never mentions the Holy Spirit.

The New Adam is going to bring us new truths for a new age and we can throw our New Testaments away, Moon indicates. We should have thrown our Old Testaments away long ago, according to Moon's view of this age. Jesus was supposed to have brought new truths which nullified the ''old'' ones. Yet Christianity began with the Old Testament, and Jesus Himself and all of His apostles referred only to the Old Testament when they spoke of ''the scriptures.'' Christians still use both Testaments as one Bible, of course.

The point isn't worth arguing except to notice that the Word of God is being defamed, a hallmark of false prophets through the ages.

The idea of Jesus and His disciples waiting in Paradise for men to finish bringing in the Kingdom is as offensive as it is ungodly. Moon fails to appreciate that God is timeless and that it is men who live in time and think of things as ''future''. The picture of a powerless, waiting Jesus is as repelling as that of a pitiable God. Moon recklessly goes wherever his philosophy takes him, and we are seeing what complex inanities result when one first departs from the Word.

Moon's constant emphasis on the need for Christians to accept his new messiah speaks loudly of who he thinks his enemies are. There is something very defamatory about his unremitting suggestions that Christians will be the ones standing in the way of the new age; Christians will be the ones who repeat the Jewish mistakes (in *this* speech at least); and Christians are the ones who'd better watch out in the coming judgment.

When it suits Moon he is a Christian. He is *Reverend*

Moon, after all, though the facts about his ordination are never mentioned. But when it suits Moon's purposes of oratory, he becomes somewhat anti-Christian. Probably he knows there is a danger of some of his listeners simply turning to a solid Christian church which studies the Bible to get the truth. He would certainly lose them then. It's better for him to color Christians red, for devils.

A CHEAP TICKET

The sheep and goats judgment (Matt. 25) is at least at the right time—the beginning of the Kingdom—but Moon confuses it with the Day of the Lord, ''Judgment Day'' (Rev. 20). Most biblically unread people don't realize the difference and Moon has a wonderful message that they love to hear—God is not going to bring fire, destroy the world, or anything like it. With Moon you can get out of all that, here and now. Just listen to his ''truth.''

Going with Moon, then, is a sort of escape for those who know very well that they have never gone with God. The soothing message of a new prophet is a lot easier to deal with than the rather more difficult message of the Bible, and those who don't understand salvation are easily taken in. With Moon, who is there to see and touch, you can get a ticket to the Kingdom very cheaply, and God's oldtime admonitions are nullified.

Give me that old-time religion.

Moon's one-world civilization of the future, which involves combining America and the Orient, is a rather self-serving ideal of his. The Eastern view of the West seems always to be that we over here are materialistic and unspiritual. We should combine our scientific know-how with the real spiritual stuff of the mysterious East.

A truer picture of things spiritual is that the West has followed the Bible and the East has gone off into cults and paganism. The West may have had the advantage, as the Apostles primarily went into Western civilizations with the gospel, but we have subsequently sent missionaries of our own throughout the world. We cannot claim that everything in American civilization is pleasing to God, but neither is the West unspiritual and in need of rejuvenation from The Orient. It has ever been the other way around.

Rather, biblically oriented people will realize that Moon is again plugging his worldwide religion system, more characteristic of the antichrist's civilization than of the Kingdom of God. Many things Moon says smack of the coming tribulation period and the new order to be established by the antichrist, and that becomes plainer as his "theology" progresses.

Probably Christian readers are thirsty at this point for a little of the real Word of God. We will take up now, by way of contrast, the way God, rather than Moon, pictures things to come.

Chapter Six

The Future,
According To God

The Future, According to God

In a way, God and Moon agree on the future. The Bible outlines a future for men which dovetails surprisingly well with many of Rev. Moon's fondest dreams.

The problem is, what Moon regards as ultimate triumph—world unity, a new Messiah, men establishing their own Kingdom on earth—ties in with the most dire warnings in God's Word. Truly, Rev. Moon seems to be working for the wrong side in the spiritual struggle between God and Satan.

MOON'S RELIGION

Rev. Moon's religion embraces three major doctrines—sinless perfection of the believers here and now; world unity, religious and political; and the worship of man, whether Moon himself or the Lord of the Second Advent. Almost all that he preaches falls under one or another of these basic doctrines.

No Christian doctrine of this age falls under any of those categories, though Moon of course professes Christianity.

PERFECTION OF THE BELIEVERS

Moonies are required to be sinless, utterly and completely. There are punishments for the least hint of sin or doubt in the Moonie movement, as we will see in the first-person testimony later in this chapter. Moon says of himself, "He (God) is living in me and I am the incarnation of Himself,"* and therefore those following Moon are, in effect, working directly with God. They must therefore be perfect.

No other religion seems to require perfection of the believers, least not of all Christianity. The Bible is very clear on the sinful condition of all men; the death of Christ was required for the forgiveness of men. Christians hold that men are to be pardoned, not perfected by their own efforts. Salvation is the free gift of God, "lest any man boast" (Eph. 2:8-9), in the way Moon often boasts about his own purity. Christians realize, from the scriptures, that they shall not reach perfection until the return of Jesus Christ (Phil. 1:6).

But Moon does away with Christianity in some of his teaching. "God is now throwing Christianity away and is now establishing a new religion, and this new religion is Unification Church," he says. "All the Christians in the world are destined to be absorbed by our movement . . . There have been saints, prophets, many religious leaders . . . Master (Moon) here is more than any of those people and greater than Jesus himself."

Moon gathers a great many converts by his false promises of sinlessness, and he scares people by accusing them of not really loving God. Interestingly the scriptures characterize Satan as the accuser of the saints (Job, e.g.). Actually, God is much more realistic about the human condition than Moon., "All sin and fall short of the glory of God," the Bible says (Rom. 3:23) and so God has made a New Covenant with men to "forgive their iniquities and remember their sins no more" (Jer. 31:34). The blood of Christ washes away the sins of the believers (Matt. 26:28) and that is the New Testament in its simplest terms.

---

* All quotes in this chapter reprinted by permission from *Time*, The Weekly Newsmagazine; copyright *Time Inc.*, unless otherwise specified in the text.

If we could be sinless with Moon we would have no need of Christ, and that is the idea behind the Unification Church. That people believe Moon shows that the Bible is not understood and large groups of men are still looking for a new savior.

WORLD UNITY

The heart of Moon's American philosophy is that from this powerful, wealthy nation the world can be conquered for Moon. He is remarkably candid on his plans, at least to Moonie listeners: ''The whole world is in my hand, and I will conquer and subjugate the world'' (as he was accurately quoted by the interviewed Moonie mother in the National Observer, chapter 5.)

The Time article we have quoted previously provided a lengthy quotation of Moon's world unity plans in rather frightening terms:

> Once our movement arouses the interest of the people in a nation, through its mass media it will spread all throughout the world . . . So, we are going to focus our attention on one nation from where to reach the world. For that purpose I chose the U.S..

> The present United Nations must be annihilated by our power. That is the stage for the Communists. We must make a new U.N..

> If the U. S. continues its corruption, and we find among the Senators and Congressmen no one really usable for our purposes, we can make Senators and Congressmen out of our members . . . I have met many famous, so-called famous, Senators and Congressmen; but to

my eyes they are just nothing. They are weak and helpless. We will win the battle. This is our dream, our project. But shut your mouth tight.

Biblically read Christians immediately recognize talk of world unity as a characteristic of the Tribulation Period. In the seven-year Tribulation to be undergone before the return of Christ to the earth, the world *will* be unified, but under the antichrist.

There is not sufficient space to fully develop the spectre of world unity and all of its evils here. The reader is referred to Hal Lindsey's definitive ''The Late, Great Planet Earth,'' or ''Satan in the Sanctuary,'' by the author and Dr. Thomas S. McCall. Moon likes to speak of world unity as the happy union of peoples of all races and nationalities, but this will be possible only in the Kingdom as established by Christ Himself, after the Tribulation Period. Prophecy is very clear on this future issue.

The antichrist's unity of the world will be a dictatorship based on a personality cult, not unlike Unification Church. For the short period of seven years the world will be duped into following a false ''messiah'' motivated by Satan himself (Rev. 13). The return of Christ will stop this heinous apostasy, which will have led the nations of the world into Armageddon, a far cry from the unity dreamed about by Rev. Moon.

WORSHIPING A MAN

If it seems surprising that people can be made to worship a man, one has only to sample Moon's claims about himself. We have seen above that he feels that he is the incarnation of God Himself, and greater than Jesus. His pronouncements to the Moonies are given under the herald of MASTER SPEAKS!

Hear his astounding self-deification:

> I am a thinker, I am your brain.

> When you join the effort with me, you can do everything in utter obedience to me. Because what I am doing is not done at random but what I am doing is under God's command.

> There is no complaint, objection to anything being done here until we will have established the Kingdom of God on earth up until the very end! There can *never* be any complaint! (Emphasis Moon's).

> I want to have the members under me who will be willing to obey me even though they may have to disobey their own parents and the Presidents of their own nations. And if I gain half the population of the world, I can turn the whole world upside down.

> You must start over again your new life, from that point denying your past families, friends, neighbors and relatives.

> (All quoted from same Time article)

This overwhelmingly dictatorial language might remind one of the past, of Hitler or Caesar, but it more pointedly tells of the future when the antichrist will demand such mindless, fanatical worship. Paul reveals that the antichrist will actually enter the Temple of God, then to be rebuilt in Jerusalem, and declare that he *is* God:

Let no man deceive you by any means: for that day shall not come, except there come a falling away first, and that man of sin be revealed, the son of perdition (the antichrist); who opposeth and exalteth himself above all that is called God; so that he as God sitteth in the temple of God, showing himself that he is God (2 Thess. 2:3-4).

The antichrist is a man, not a deity or spirit-being of any sort, who carries out the work of the devil, as he is characterized in the Book of Revelation. The idea of Moon demanding the kind of reverence that he does is a definitive harbinger of the antichrist.

WHO IS MOON?

To some people Moon is the antichrist, plain and simple. He has not yet come to full power but the Tribulation Period situations are not quite established yet either. He seems to be here, right on time and acting his role according to prophecy.

But to place this horrible mantle on any man is certainly a serious charge, and Moon has not thus far claimed to be a world deliverer. He has reserved that role for his Lord of the Second Advent, though many have called him that as well.

Moon *has* claimed to be a prophet for our time, and people have thought of him as the False Prophet of Rev. 19:20 and 20:10. The False Prophet is the herald and helper of the antichrist. But the False Prophet is a worker of miracles and Moon's work falls far short from what anyone would term a miracle. Perhaps he will show more thrilling stuff as his ministry progresses, but thus far he doesn't look very supernatural at all.

As far as Moon being a "Messiah," he *has* claimed *this* on occasion and the Moonies firmly claim it for him (though not in initiation lectures such as the one I underwent). But the term "messiah" can be slippery. It literally means "anointed one," or more figuratively, one called to a purpose by God. Cyrus of Persia is an anointed of God in scripture since he carries out the purposes of God (Isa. 45:1). Moon can claim messiahship on the basis of his interviews with God, et. al., and still give way to his Lord of the Second Advent.

Prophet or messiah, Moon's doctrine is seen to be false when held up to the light of scripture, and we have quoted throughout this book Jesus' admonitions of such characters coming on the scene in the end times (Mt. 24:24, e.g.). Moon's claims are more all-embracing than those of other cultists generally; Mahareshi Mahesh Yogi, the guru of transcendental meditation, seems to promise only a relaxing time through his westernized Hinduism, and Maharaj Ji seems content to shed his Divine Light in rather limited, local circumstances.

Moon is out to conquer the world, and this puts him in a class by himself among "prophets."

The majority of Moon watchers consider him either a deluded semi-Christian pastor or a simple secular opportunist. The *Jewish Digest* of June, 1976 characterizes him as "an Oriental Elmer Gantry," but those investigating his financial successes see him as more of a small-time sharpie.

Whoever he really is—however he might fit into prophecy and however important a place he may have—Moon should never be sold short. He is amazingly wealthy and powerful, he is skillful at religion and its attraction for lost people, and he is heartless in his ambition. Given enough leeway to carry forth his international projects, Moon can mean real trouble for a great many people—especially young people.

Most youngsters who get caught up with Moon's dogma haven't any conception of what they are getting into, of course. In the manner of Cynthia Slaughter, they believe one lie at a time until they are hooked. It is only after certain Moonies leave the movement and come back to normal life that they give awesome testimony of what really goes on in the Unification Church.

In the following section is a testimony so overwhelmingly tragic, so shockingly repulsive, that it will be hard to believe even for those who fully understand the dangers of false religions. It answers better the question, "Who is Moon?" than all the biblical analysis in the world, and it happened to a 16 year-old girl.

"Why I Quit

the Moon Cult"

The true seventeen-month experience of a teen-age girl,
who was first drawn to, then repelled by
the strange world of the Unification Church

Over a million young men and women hungering
for a new faith have been recruited in recent years
into more than 1,800 extremist and mystic religious
cults in the United States. The largest cult is
believed to be the Unification Church, headed by a
fifty-six-year-old Korean immigrant who calls himself the Reverend Sun Myung Moon. The UC boasts
30,000 American members, nicknamed "Moonies," a
third of whom live full-time in communes scattered
across the country. Since his arrival in 1972, Moon
has become the focus of growing controversy. Many
former followers, angry parents, traditional religious
leaders and independent investigators accuse
him—and the heads of other cults—of using
brainwashing and mind control to win and exploit
converts. Currently several congressional commit-
tees are probing such operations. What follows are
the true experiences, as told to writers Charles and
Bonnie Remsberg, of one teen-age girl who joined,
then quit the Moon movement.

My teeth are chattering. But I have to keep singing—a sobbing, hoarse squawking, really—because that's all that keeps me from screaming. For nearly half an hour I've stood in the shower while icy water has peppered my body. I tried jogging in place in a frantic effort to keep warm, but an agonizing numbness quickly took over. Now I've begun to jerk uncontrollably. And I still have four freezing hours to go to fulfill my punishment. If I fail, I believe with all my heart that Satan will "invade" me. Warmth is just a footstep away, out of these relentless jets of frigid water, but I am terrified to take it . . .

Moments like that seem unreal to me now. But as a follower of the Reverend Sun Myung Moon, I meekly performed many strange and painful chores. At times, I could scarcely believe these things were happening to *me.* Yet, as desperately as I wanted to escape this bizarre life, I stayed because of a force beyond my control.

I was sixteen when I first encountered the Moon cult. I was a junior at a Catholic girls' high school in Long Island, New York, an honors student, on excellent terms with my parents, straight, together. When I finally left it seventeen months later, I was literally insane.

Only recently, after months of therapy, was I discharged from a mental hospital in New England, where I had been locked in a bare room in the violent ward; at times, I had not recognized my own mother.

Details of some of my experiences are still blocked from my mind. But as a part of getting well I have managed to relive most of what I went through, to try to understand how it happened.

Some of the memories are of things so *right*—unless I could have predicted where they would lead. Like the beginning . . .

December 1973. Bitter cold. I'm running down the steps of the public library in midtown Manhattan with a girl friend, when a young man, about twenty-two, looking half-frozen, approaches. Clean shaven, short blond hair, old-fashioned clothes like the kind my father would wear—not at all a hippy or drug-freak type. He's from a "training program," he says.

I don't ordinarily strike up conversations with strangers, but my friend seems intrigued by him. She urges that we accept his invitation to a coffee shop across the street.

He chats amiably about college (he's a pre-med dropout), a cheese-tasting party he went to, the ballet, our diets. Honest. Open. Religion? "I don't go for the blind faith bit, because it doesn't seem logical or sensible," I remark. "I believe in God, but religion's no big thing in my life." He seems annoyed but smiles and talks with great enthusiasm about some "fascinating" Oriental people he has met. Before we rush off, we promise to join him next weekend at a lecture.

My girl friend can't make it, so I go alone to the lecture site, a townhouse on Manhattan's Upper East Side. The minute I'm in the door, people swarm over me, college-age kids mostly, shaking my hand, praising me. I'm "love-bombed"!

The lecture's weird. Some Japanese guy with a terrible language problem drones on for hours. The other kids sit enthralled. Over and over he mentions the Reverend Sun Myung Moon. A girl points to an enormous blow-up photo covering almost an entire wall: That's him.

The lectures seem boring, but the young people I meet are so appealing that I'm back the next week. And the next. I know now this is a center for the Unification Church that Moon heads. Many of the kids live here. Everyone tells me Moon is the Messiah, that he's higher than Jesus, that God speaks to him and wants him to rule the world. What *I* dig are these outgoing people. Clean-cut. Happy all the time. No displays of anger or snobbishness.

I'm fond of Pam. She's twenty-seven, in the group two years, not quite like a mother but not quite like a peer either. We eat together; she walks me to the bus stop to be sure I get home safely.

My parents are hassling me about spending so much time at the center and coming home late. But this is an adventure, something I can be involved in independent of my school and family, a different world that's *mine*. I like it because it's something my classmates aren't into.

To keep my friendships going I have to concentrate on the lectures, which mix politics, history and the Bible together, seeming always to prove that Rev. Sun Myung Moon is God's chosen messenger, someone who *must* be followed to save oneself and one's descendants from eternal hell. These lectures seem to fit everything together so logically, leaving nothing to question. That appeals to my intellect. I don't really know enough about history and politics—or religion either—to detect any distortions or errors of fact.

I'm such a "good person" that Pam arranges private lectures for me. We go to a room with velvet seats and sofas, thick carpeting, a chandelier. The same Japanese man (a scientist, I'm told) drills me week after week on messages found in the Bible and in history, and the point of each message seems to be Moon. I hear it all so often that I'm beginning to believe it.

Any talk of my outside world turns Pam off. I want

desperately to please her. I drop my boy-friend because Pam says, "You don't need him to be a complete person." My friends at school fade away. Pam is pleased at my attention to Rev. Moon. When we're together, we kneel and pray to his picture.

June 1974. My grandmother is crying. My parents are at work, and she knows I'm getting ready to leave forever.

The hassling has become intolerable: Why can't I be a Christian in my own church (meaning *their* church)? They don't understand. I've come to believe that there's so much sin in all of us to fight against! I go days without eating, until I'm dizzy and faint. I take freezing showers and rack my brain for ways to inflict pain on myself. Women are supposed to feel pain and suffering for the pain Eve caused God, the lectures say; I believe that now. Pam says my parents *can't* understand because they are agents of Satan. They've ordered me to stop going to the center. But through my lessons there I have come to believe that I am a *very* special person in my family—as if my whole history has been shaped so I can serve the Lord through Rev. Moon.

I need only attend a summer session to graduate from high school a year ahead of schedule. Pam says that's a temptation by Satan to divert me from important work. I want to do good for the world, and I believe I can do it best by helping advance the cause of Rev. Moon.

I slam the door on my grandmother's sobs. By nightfall, inside the center, its doors closed against a hostile world, I am a full-fledged, full-time Moonie. My *true* parents now are the Reverend Sun Myung Moon and his wife.

My world is turned upside down. From the instant I commit my life to Rev. Moon, the atmosphere changes drastically. I'm flown with fifteen others to a communal center in Los Angeles, the location unknown to my mother and father. Pam is 2,500 miles behind in New York. My shoulder-length hair is chopped into a pixie by other Moonies to discourage vanity. Makeup is forbidden. I'm ordered to dress modestly, in hand-me-down skirt and blouse and knee socks. The aura of warm acceptance that surrounded the lectures and drills is supplanted by an exhausting, rigid routine.

Like thousands of Moonies across the country, I work all day, every day, selling carnations to raise money for the movement. Up at 4:00 a.m. Rattling through the streets with other teams in a seatless van by 5:00, heading for shopping centers or business districts. Breakfast is Chinese rice balls or cereal and candy served in the van, milk spilling all over.

Team captains whip us into an evangelical frenzy with songs, Bible verses, prayers, chants. We each call out our "determination"—the amount we vow we'll personally raise that day. No one shouts out an amount less than $100. Some caught up in the moment scream, "*$1,000!*"

On the streets until the money is made, no matter how long it takes. Rarely back before midnight or 1:00 a.m. Dinner—vegetables, starches, no meat. Often too beat to eat. Testimonials about interesting experiences of the day, with emphasis on visions and mystical revelations of Rev. Moon. More Bible, more drumming about Moon as Messiah, more singing to "drive away evil spirits." Collapse in sleep until the next day begins before dawn.

All emotion—everything—is handled by the center director. If I sing too loud, he tells me how to sing. If I want to eat or sit with different people, he says no. If I feel like crying, he snaps, "Don't cry tears for yourself." There are no newspapers, no TV, no talk of the outside world.

Only later, after I have left the cult, will I see what's happening here. The "warm" kids in New

York fear showing any other emotion because they have been made to believe that "negative" thoughts are a sign that the devil has invaded them. They are under great pressure to win new recruits, like me, so that they will be blessed by Rev. Moon.

Now, though I don't realize it yet, I'm being manipulated in another way. The lack of sleep, the poor food, the ceaseless noise and commotion, the isolation, the chanted prayers and songs weaken my mental resistance and make me desperately afraid of trying to break free.

I never wake without wondering what I'm doing here. But by the time the determinations are hollered out, I'm thinking only of how to sell enough flowers to meet my quota. If we don't sell more, the captains say, Rev. Moon will fail to win this country, and Satan will triumph.

Like the others, I lie. "The money goes for drug rehabilitation programs," I tell some people. Or for "Christian youth projects." Few ask for details. The flowers sell for donations of at least $1 apiece, triple their cost. Some days I raise over $240, never less than $99. I give it to the captains and never hear of it again.

On the road: We're in a caravan trying to canvass every town in California, or so it seems. One girl rents a hotel room each night. The rest of us sneak up the fire escape with our sleeping bags. The boys sleep in the vans. Sexual contact is strictly taboo, along with drinking, smoking, drugs. Male and female clothing can't even be laundered together. My legs ache from pounding the pavement. An inch-thick callus has hardened on my sole.

I'm sick. Fever. Can't get up. Other Moonies sprinkle "holy salt" around my bed to drive away "bad spirits." A doctor? Forget it. I know of one Moon girl who developed an eye ailment. Other members were brought in to see her writhing in pain—as an example of "someone who is possessed." By the time she was finally allowed to get medical treatment, she was partially blind. If you're sick, it means your ancestors sinned, and you're paying.

September 1974. Physically and emotionally drained, I'm back in New York for a new assignment: "witnessing"—winning converts.

My days, rain or shine, are spent approaching people as I was first approached at the library. I don't have a knack for spotting good prospects, as some Moonies do. Day after day, people ignore me.

I'm swept with guilts and fears. The center director tells me if I witness unsuccessfully to a girl and she's raped the next week, it's *my* fault, because I didn't bring her into the movement in time.

I'm given "conditions," or punishments, to free me of Satan's influence. Cold showers—longer and longer ones. Reading Rev. Moon's doctrines over and over. Praying all night in repentance, begging God to forgive me. Fasting a week at a time. By eagerly serving the conditions, I can overcome my sins.

Oh, God, please help me! I'm so afraid!

I'm home. After months of not knowing even whether I am alive, my mother has tracked me down. She has persuaded me to come home. I have been here for weeks, without finding the peace I crave.

My parents complain that I move and act like a zombie, kneeling in prayer hours at a time. But inside I'm churning.

Something horrible is going to happen because I left the movement. I had been warned of that certainty from the day I joined. You *hear* of terrible cases: parents dying of heart attacks, kids struck by cars and paralyzed—because a Moonie left the faith.

The pull to go back is phenomenal. I can't relate to my old friends who drop by. I can't readjust to family living. I feel guilty, nervous because everything is so good here. Once rested, I'm driven wild by the inactivity. While I sit here, Satan is tightening his grip on the world.

February 7, 1975. I flee the house and go back to the center. It's my mother's birthday.

Caldwell, New Jersey. The Moon group has arranged with authorities at a county correctional center to furnish materials with which women inmates can fashion flower arrangements in jars of colored sand, to be sold by Moonies. My job: to help supervise and convert the prisoners.

Two Moonies begin complaining the project is a rip-off. The prisoners are paid 45 cents for each jar they complete, but they sell for $5 apiece. Some of the money is supposed to go for prisoner rehabilitation, but there's no evidence that it ever does. One night the two complainers tell me our team captain gave them a car without brakes: "He wanted us to crash."

Terrible news. A young Moonie at a center in New York State takes off his clothes, lies down on a railroad track and lets a train cut off his head. We're told: "The boy was possessed."

I have doubts! But doubts are forbidden. When I try to question aloud whether I am doing right to stay here, more conditions are heaped on me.

Finally, I'm ordered to the Moon training center at Barrytown, New York, for intensified indoctrination.

Gorgeous place! $1.5 million estate, 255 acres overlooking the Hudson River. But the peaceful setting is deceptive.

I'm constantly criticized for the way I walk, talk, sit—all too sensual. I'm arrogant because I sometimes speak with my chin raised. From six o'clock in the morning until eleven at night there are lectures. At the end of each day I have to write a "reflection sheet," parroting how wonderful all the messages are. Those few who question the lectures are ostracized as negative persons.

I am lying on my bed one warm night in May 1975, exhausted, frantically worrying what will become of me. Suddenly the world goes black. I am screaming, screaming, screaming . . .

My memories of the next few weeks are only fragments. I vaguely recall being driven by jeep back to the center in Manhattan . . . being locked in a room . . . flying into uncontrollable rages . . . having my forehead rubbed with oil . . . being given drugs I cannot identify . . . trying to climb out of a high window.

By Memorial Day, the center director was so alarmed he wanted nothing more to do with me. He phoned my mother and asked her to take me home. I had to be carried to the car. During the tense ride to Long Island, I sobbed like a baby.

Doctors diagnosed me as psychotic, out of touch with reality. Under the emotional and physical pressures of the cult, my mind "just went." It took months of intense treatment to put the pieces back together again.

During my long stay in the mental hospital, I was deprogrammed from the cult's beliefs. Point by point I was shown how Rev. Moon's doctrines are based on distorted interpretations of the Bible and his own pernicious philosophy. I also learned of evidence pointing to the fact that millions of dollars collected by Moonies goes for his personal aggrandizement rather than to finance good works. Therapists explained the techniques that were used to indoctrinate me—sleep deprivation, protein-deficient food, repetitious drilling, isolation, exploitation of fear and guilt. These are the methods that have been employed to brainwash prisoners of war.

Last November I was released from the hospital, emotionally stable and cured of any desire to return to the orbit of the Reverend Sun Myung Moon. Bills for my treatment came to more than $20,000; my parents will be paying for years.

I'm a college freshman now, hoping to become a nurse or a doctor. I'm pulling an A average. Not bad for a comeback. But I feel like a plant that's been yanked out of the soil, then put back in, trying to develop roots again.

I'm different from the person I used to be. I'm more hesitant about getting into discussions, more timid about going places on my own. I'm much more dependent on my parents, emotionally and socially. As a counterreaction to caring so much about Moon, I'm completely indifferent about politics and religion. In the cult I lost confidence in myself and my abilities.

I think I'm getting more into the scene, expressing myself and what I want to be like and getting back my old belief in my ability to do things right. I don't feel comfortable with it yet, but I'm getting there.

I wonder how long it will be before I feel totally "me" again.

COPING WITH CULTS

Religious cults demanding fanatical loyalty to their leaders can represent a threat to young people.

Jean Merritt, who heads Return to Personal Choice, a counseling service for ex-cultists, says, "Idealistic young people who have many questions about life and who seek absolute answers seem most likely to get involved. Some emerge with severe mental disorders after they have been programmed to do desperate things."

Deception is often used in recruitment. Because cults often operate through fronts that appear to be discussion groups or youth clubs, young people may not realize they've been entrapped. How can you be on guard? Jean Merritt offers these suggestions:

BE SKEPTICAL of strangers who invite you to lectures, movies, workshops, retreats or other events. Ask blunt questions about their religion and philosophy. Don't accept evasive answers. Inquire how they spend their time each day, why they aren't in school or working in regular jobs.

BEWARE of groups that place heavy emphasis on fund-raising, profess utter devotion to a single leader, demand vows of poverty by full-time members and encourage a monastic life style.

BE CAUTIOUS of any group that asks you to fill out a financial statement or donate your material possessions, or warns you not to tell your parents you're involved.

BE LEERY of any communal living situation.

BE SUSPICIOUS of a "religious" group that does not meet in an established religious building of the kind with which you are familiar.

LAMBS TO THE SLAUGHTER

Not much can be added to the above testimony of grief and despair. We might only notice that this unfortunate girl was taken away by Rev. Moon because she had little to combat him with and no knowledge of what true faith amounts to. She was led like a lamb to the slaughter.

The Jewish Digest, in its investigative article about Rev. Moon, suggested that the family life of many teens today leaves spiritual gaps which cultists can rush in to fill. Writing about a reclaimed Jewish Moonie, reporter Ira Pearlstein said pointedly, " "And Karen still finds her parents' middle class values, and Judaism included, inadequate . . . Karen and her fellow ex-Moonies do not feel they have much to come home to . . . We cannot blame this on Rev. Moon. It is our doing, our responsibility to repair."

Christian youngsters as well fall prey to Moon, presumably because they feel a spiritual need and think that he can fill it. As in Pearlstein's honest appraisal of the Jewish situation, we cannot blame Rev. Moon; it is our responsibility as parents to provide an adequate Christian understanding and environment for growing youngsters.

"ASK AND IT SHALL BE GIVEN"

Christian parents and young people, and non-Christian readers alike, should understand the differences between Christianity and Rev. Moon's religion. In Moon's three major doctrines Christianity is completely opposed. We do not expect sinless perfection of the believers in the here-and-now. We try to maintain a good testimony in the course of loving and serving God, but we realize that our final perfection awaits the return of Jesus Christ. We are not striving for world unity of any kind, nor making an effort in our own strength to bring in the Kingdom of Heaven. God will act to accomplish both of those in His own providence. And finally, and most importantly, we do not worship a man—not now nor later. We worship God as always, and we shall worship the King when He returns to establish the Kingdom. Christians never give the sort of brainless adherence to a human being that Moon requires of his followers; and we do not make obeisances to pictures, look for new information from God through a latter day prophet, nor believe that we shall be sanctified by a man in the flesh.

Christianity is simply not a system of works done to cajole God into having mercy on us. God has already said that He will have mercy on us—indeed He will honor us—when we become followers of His Son. And He made provision for that to be elegantly simple.

"Ask and it shall be given," God said.
"Seek and ye shall find."
"Knock and it will be opened unto you."

Many people do not become followers of Jesus because they do not realize that the door is truly open and that God has expressed His will plainly on this. Moon by and large attracts people of no religion at all, and they have no faith because they have not comprehended that true faith is easy to have. God gives it, freely. It has been already paid for, in effect, by the atoning death of Christ.

Instead of people following every cultist that comes along, giving up their families and fortunes to miserable systems of pagan lies, it should be realized that the door to the 2,000 year-old Christian church remains open today. In the words of Moon, God has worked a long time toward this situation. Since Abraham and God's covenant with him, the Almighty has made every effort to guarantee that all men might come home to Him, might be truly perfected, might have the Kingdom of Heaven on earth and might become truly one nation under God.

Truly, and it can't be said more simply, the way to God is open, and all that Rev. Moon promises in his wildest rantings about salvation, is free for the asking.